EDUCATION ON SITF

A TEACHER'S GUIDE TO
GEOGRAPHY AND THE HISTORIC ENVIRONMENT

Tim Copeland

English # Heritage

English # Heritage

GEOGRAPHY AND THE HISTORIC ENVIRONMENT

CONTENTS

ABOUT THIS BOOK 3

LOOKING AT THE ENVIRONMENT 4
What is the historic environment?
A dynamic environment
Questions and the historic environment

GEOGRAPHICAL SKILLS AND SOURCES 7
Maps, plans, aerial photographs
Sites and Monuments Records
Fieldwork skills and soil, geology and weather

SITES IN THE PRESENT LANDSCAPE 10
A case study of a rural area

SITES AND VISITS 12
Which sites to visit?

DEFENSIVE SITES 13
Hill forts
Roman forts
Castles
Pillboxes

CEREMONIAL AND RELIGIOUS SITES 18
Prehistoric ceremonial sites
Churches
Abbeys

INDUSTRIAL SITES 22
Prehistoric industrial sites
Sites of the industrial revolution

SETTLEMENT SITES 25
Village
Town

CHANGE AND THE HISTORIC ENVIRONMENT 29
Elements of the past
The influence of the past
Links with other places
The changing environment

BIBLIOGRAPHY AND RESOURCES 35
Acknowledgements

Tunbridge Wells Museum and Art Gallery

GEOGRAPHY AND THE HISTORIC ENVIRONMENT

ABOUT THIS BOOK

Geography is about place, and the relationship between people and the environment that shapes what a place is like and how it works. In England almost every locality has evidence remaining of how people in the past interacted with the place to give it the characteristics that we see today. We call this evidence the historic environment. The challenge is to use these places to enable children to understand the impact and influence which people in the past have had on the present environment.

This book will explore individual sites and local landscapes. It will also demonstrate how a range of geographical skills may be developed through working with the historic environment.

The main focus will be on activities that children can undertake when exploring their local landscape or visiting a historic monument or site. Several sites have been selected as detailed case studies throughout the book. The suggested activities in each case study may be adapted for work at other sites including the immediate locality of the school.

This book aims to:

■ show how our present landscape is a product of the past.

■ show how to look at the individual historic components of the landscape to see how they survive today and how they functioned in the past.

■ discuss the sources and skills that may be used to help us to understand places.

■ consider the various needs of historic places today and some of the tensions that may arise between these needs.

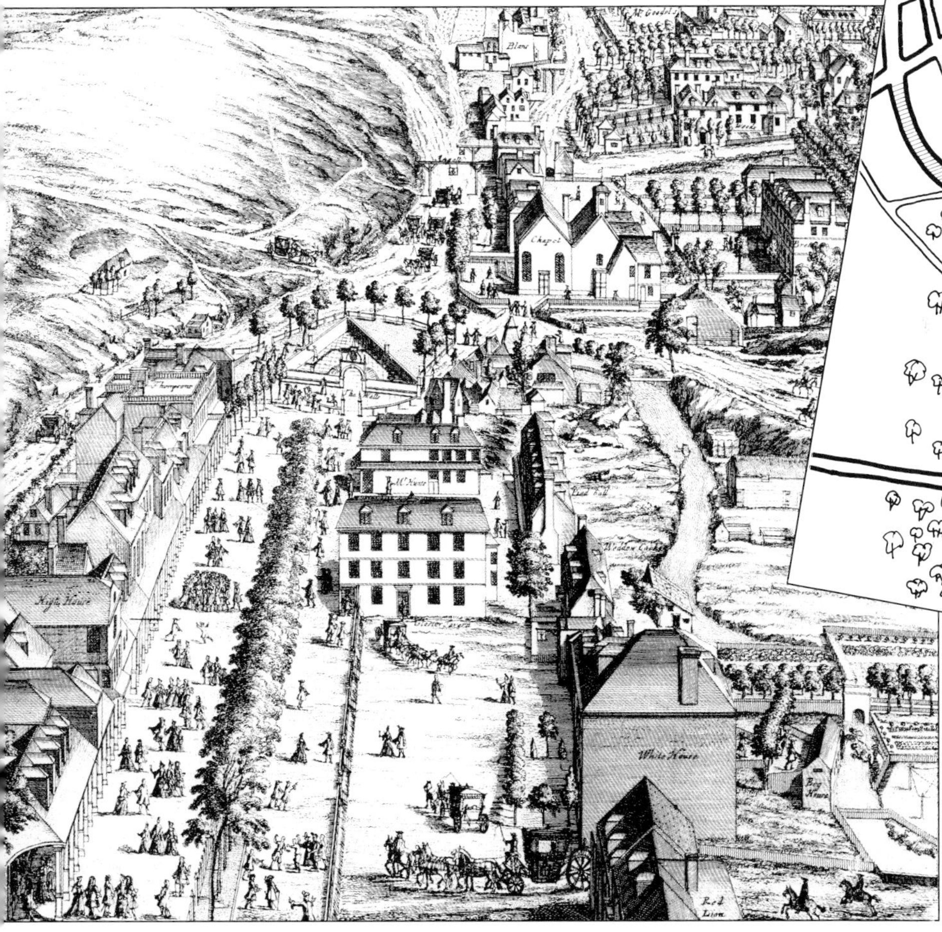

An engraving of Tunbridge Wells in 1719. Comparison with a present day map of the area clearly shows the almost unchanged road layout, as indicated by shaded areas.

GEOGRAPHY AND THE HISTORIC ENVIRONMENT

LOOKING AT THE ENVIRONMENT

WHAT IS THE HISTORIC ENVIRONMENT?

The historic environment was created by past human activity and might be a village, a town, or an area of rural landscape. Human activity had an impact on the physical environment long before written historical records began, and a lot may be learned by looking at prehistoric sites. Some historic features may be buried below the ground or water and already known to archaeologists, or they may await discovery and identification. The common factor is that all these features survive from previous times and exert some influence, even though it may be hidden, on the present environment.

The historic environment lies all around us; what varies is the extent to which it appears within today's environment and how far we are able to recognise it. Nearly all places in England, whether urban or rural, upland or lowland, industrial or agricultural, contain evidence of some aspect of human activity in the past. In many places there is obvious evidence of the past in the buildings and structures of the town and city, village and farmland. For example in a town such as York or Canterbury, shape, function and character are immediately seen as a product of the past. In other towns evidence is equally abundant but may be hidden, and techniques such as fieldwork, research, surveying and excavation will be needed to find the clues. Many modern rural parish boundaries are evidence for Saxon trackways or Roman estate boundaries whose lines they still follow, and many a garden boundary in a modern housing estate is the survival of an ancient hedgeline. Even new towns such as Milton Keynes have been shown to lie over extensive evidence of human occupation that is thousands of years old, and the shape of those historic landscapes has influenced some aspects of the shape of the present urban landscape.

The sites described in the following pages have been chosen for their accessibility, but it is important that children understand that the historic environment is all around them.

A DYNAMIC ENVIRONMENT

The historic environment is dynamic, it has changed greatly and continues to change. Features from many periods of the past can be found at the same location, the result of physical and human activity over thousands of years. A locality often shows continuity of occupation from earliest times to the present day.

From the earliest period of the human occupation of Britain, human beings have changed the natural landscape of the country as they sought to modify it for their own ends. This activity, closely related to human needs, has resulted in a variety of structures for the purpose of shelter, defence, worship, agriculture or industry. Often we find all of these functions in one place or in one area in the form of farms or villages or towns. Over a period of several thousand years the purpose of these structures has remained basically the same, but as technology has developed so has the sophistication of the structures. The function of

The industrial landscape: Ironbridge (above) in Shropshire and the British Waterways building in Nottingham. The links between transport networks and the location of industry may be explored in the pupil's own locality.

LOOKING AT THE ENVIRONMENT

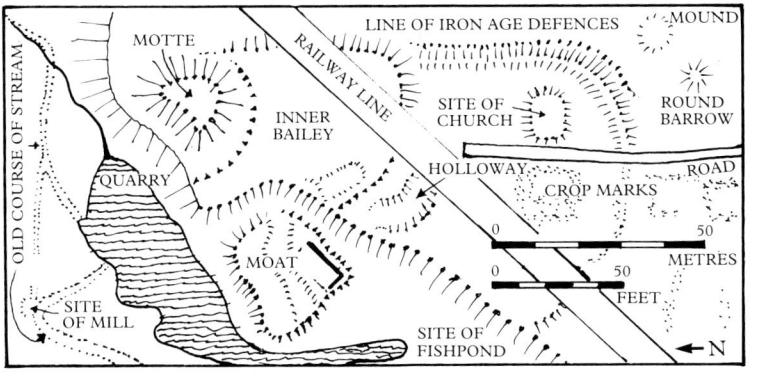

The two-dimensional landscape.

– The horizontal dimension.

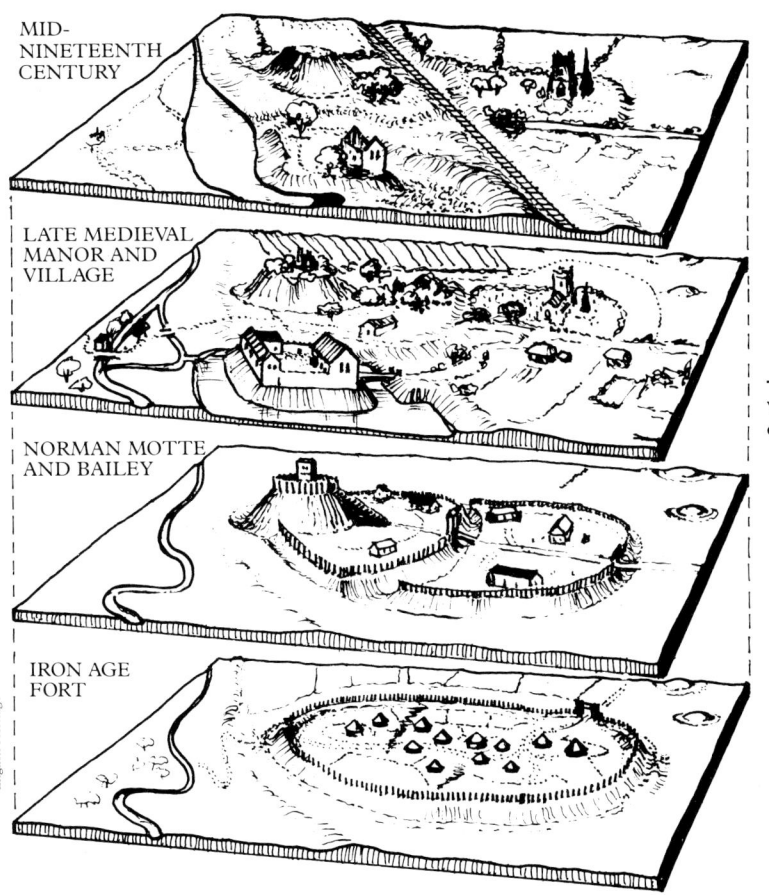

– The vertical dimension.

The historic landscape has two dimensions. This diagram shows the relationship between the vertical element of the landscape as it changed over time, and the horizontal aspect which shows the shape of the whole landscape at one particular time, either in the past or present.

eighteenth centuries. The villages that have survived have continued to develop up to the present.

Throughout the past there has been a steady drift towards urbanisation resulting in the greater part of the population of England living in towns in the present century. In the later bronze age and iron ages the first attempts at urbanisation can be seen with the growth of hill forts, and later of small towns, such as Colchester and St. Albans.

The Roman period saw the growth of many towns and a large number of these sites have remained as significant settlement points in the landscape up until the present day. In Saxon times burgs developed: settlements defended by earth and timber banks, some on sites not previously occupied, others on the sites of decayed Roman towns. The Normans in their turn developed towns which we often recognise by the presence of a castle and cathedral. Although Roman and Saxon sites were often used as the focus of Norman towns, many were built at new sites.

These towns continued to develop during the medieval and post-medieval periods. The industrial revolution provided the impetus for many new towns and cities in areas that had previously been occupied only by villages, the raw materials needed for the new factories being the main factor in the choice of location.

Continuous, or sequent, occupation of a settlement gives it a composite structure in terms of the age of its buildings. For example within the medieval walls resting on Roman town wall foundations and alongside the medieval castle and cathedral will be found medieval parish churches, post-Reformation chapels, houses which are clearly medieval in structure, Regency buildings, Victorian, Edwardian, 1930s and modern structures. There may be traces of medieval industry in the names of the streets, and both early Industrial Revolution and more modern industrial developments may be seen.

many of the structures being built today is similar to that of those that were erected in Roman towns, but the detail of the way the buildings work is very different.

In rural areas archaeologists have found evidence of isolated settlement with single or small groups of buildings at the close of the neolithic period. Rural settlements tended to develop into a pattern of farmsteads and hamlets during the bronze age and iron ages. In the Roman period of rural settlement, villas and villages became more common. It was during the Saxon and Norman periods that large numbers of villages appeared. Not all of these settlements survived. Many of them disappeared as a result of depopulation following the Black Death in the fourteenth century, or as a consequence of the enclosure movement in the fifteenth century. Others fell victim to the making of large parks attached to country houses in the seventeenth and

LOOKING AT THE ENVIRONMENT

Key questions about a place		
Present	Past	Influence of the past on the present
What is this place like?	What was this place like?	What elements of the past can we see in this place?
Why is this place as it is, how and why does it differ from or resemble other places?	Why was this place as it was, how and why did it differ from or resemble other places?	What influence have these elements had on this place, and how does this influence differ from or resemble what has happened at other places?
In what way is this place connected with other places?	In what ways was this place connected to other places?	In what ways have past connections influenced how this place is now connected with other places?
How is this place changing and why?	How did this place change and why?	How did this place change and why and how are those changes reflected in the present?
What would it feel like to be in this place?	What would it have felt like to be in this place?	How does the past influence what it feels like to be in this place?

The survival of each succeeding landscape depends on a number of factors, including the type of material being used to build the structures and the rate of agricultural, industrial and urban change. At any particular place, some structures from the past are likely still to be in use, though not necessarily for their original purpose. More recent structures might encapsulate some of the fabric of an older building. Many buildings and structures will have disappeared from above the surface of the land altogether and the only traces we will find will be below the ground, or by studying old maps, aerial photographs or other documentary evidence. Many of those sites which now leave few traces on the surface will have been destroyed only in the very recent past as more intensive agriculture and urban expansion have made an impact on the landscape.

QUESTIONS AND THE HISTORIC ENVIRONMENT

A major factor in the study of place is the influence of human behaviour on the natural characteristics of a locality, and how it contributes to a place's personality, as well as how the natural environment influences human behaviour in that locality. In studying places, and the interaction between place and human activity, children should be encouraged to ask questions. By using a set of carefully structured key questions as a starting-point, children will be able to pose their own questions at a particular site.

In order to answer these questions the elements of human, physical and environmental geography need to be focused on a locality. The result, in Britain, would be a varied picture of a specific environment, but with human activity as the major feature.

These are the key questions that will be used in this book when we are reconstructing how a place functioned in the past. Each question can generate other questions of the same type. For example 'What was this place like?' prompts further questions:

■ Where was it sited?

■ How does it fit into the physical landscape?

■ How many structures were there? What were they made of? What were they used for?

■ How many people lived here?

In many ways the organisation of the questions is cumulative in that they each build on the information and analysis of the previous question with 'What was this place like?' being the main data-collecting, fieldwork oriented, starting-point. Although these sets of questions are posed discretely here, they are interrelated. However, whilst each set of questions depends on the others, using them discretely does help to focus the stages of an enquiry. Questions like these can be used with children of all ages. With very young children the teacher is likely to pose the questions, whereas older children should be able to devise their own questions about a particular site. The activities which result from asking such questions will involve various levels of skill in observation, recording, analysis, synthesis and presentation.

GEOGRAPHY AND THE HISTORIC ENVIRONMENT

GEOGRAPHICAL SKILLS AND SOURCES

The historic environment is a rich context in which to develop the skills needed in learning geography. Just as geographical skills enable children to make sense of the present landscape, such skills are also needed to make sense of the historic environment. The historic environment could form the sole focus of a scheme of work, for example the use of a castle site to develop mapping and planning skills. An alternative approach would be to use a castle as one type of structure and land use, as part of a settlement study.

MAPS

Much analysis and recording of the historic environment relies on the use of maps, thus developing mapping and surveying skills. Finding and evaluating the location of a site to be visited will involve work with Ordnance Survey maps which will help develop the understanding of symbols, scale, purpose, and interpretation. A site's grid reference and the shape of the land around it may be determined before the fieldwork begins. Children can also make their own maps or add detail to outline maps whilst on site. Maps showing the main physical features of an area can be used to prompt discussion about suitable locations for fortifications or settlements. Specialist maps produced by the Ordnance Survey will also be useful in finding the distribution of sites of a particular period such as Ancient Britain or Roman Britain, or a particular feature such as Hadrian's Wall or an historic town.

Maps made at different times in the past are very useful for investigating the environment at the time that the map was compiled. Early county maps are almost three-dimensional in their depiction of hills and settlements and are accessible to young children who have difficulty in using two-dimensional map representations with contours. The Tithe Commutation Act of 1836 resulted in parishes being surveyed to a large scale. The maps produced give much information about land ownership, tenancy, land use and value, and field names and show in detail a landscape before the effects of the agricultural and industrial changes of the nineteenth and twentieth centuries. The first edition of the Ordnance Survey's one-inch map, which was produced in 1801, and the unbroken succession of maps to the present day give plenty of scope for comparison of land use.

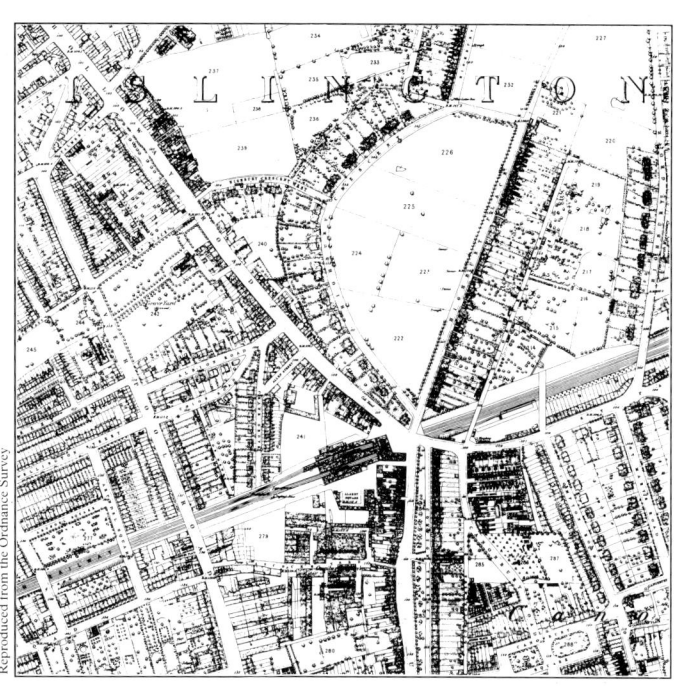

Extract from the 1871 Ordnance Survey map of Islington.

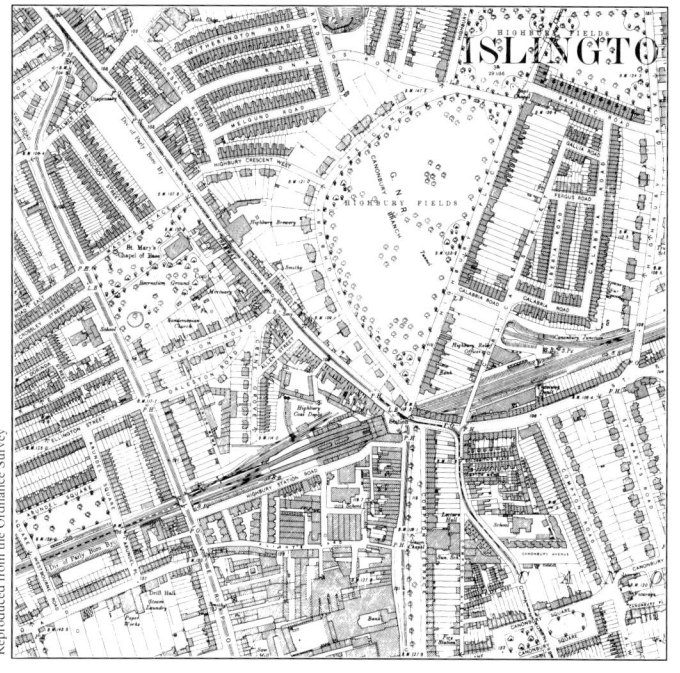

Extract from the 1894 Ordnance Survey map of Islington. Comparison of the two maps shows the extent of building work in parts of London at the end of the 19th century. Much of this development was related to the expansion of the railway system.

GEOGRAPHICAL SKILLS AND SOURCES

The problems of accuracy of old maps, their dates and the features they show or omit can usefully be built into the learning process.

It should be possible to use old maps of the locality to:

■ find when the school first appears, and the previous land use.

■ look for the children's houses. Who lives in the oldest, who in the newest? Find the changes in the way to school over a period of time.

■ determine the changes in the transport network and the growth of an area.

■ see the development in mapping techniques and symbolism.

PLANS

Many historical and archaeological sites have excellent and accurate plans available, usually in a guidebook. Where a site comprises only the bases of walls or lines in concrete or gravel showing the position of a former or buried wall the remains themselves form an obvious plan. Sites and structures from all periods can provide contrasting subject matter to the plans of the child's house or school. Castles and churches, prehistoric earthworks, deserted medieval villages, country house gardens, bridges, old factories and industrial areas as well as old farm buildings indicate the range and complexity of structures. Planning by children will develop understanding of location, perspective, style, position and orientation, direction and distance.

Not all plans are the product of recent times and at some sites plans drawn from an earlier time may survive which can be compared with the present-day layout to identify continuity and change in the site. Early plans (if accompanied by a scale) can be compared with modern ones and distances (such as the length of a wall or the circumference of a keep) can be measured on site and compared for accuracy.

Site Plan: Deal Castle.

Plan showing school buildings and play areas (below).

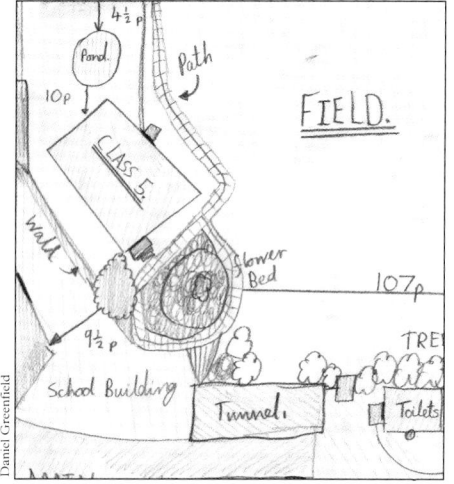

AERIAL PHOTOGRAPHS

Aerial photographs are an invaluable aid to understanding the historic environment whether they show a landscape or a single building. There are two types of aerial photograph, oblique and vertical. Verticals give a 'photographic map' of the landscape whilst obliques give a bird's-eye view. One importance of aerial photographs is that they show crop and soil marks which may indicate buried features in the landscape. Some photographs also show the shadows of slight earthworks early in the morning or in the evening sunshine. Similar effects can be seen under a light dusting of snow. These photographs can be essential in identifying some hidden or almost-hidden features of the historic environment. Photographs of the landscape have been taken from the air since the 1930s and from 1945 most areas will be covered by a series of photographs taken at regular intervals, mainly for planning purposes. If aerial photographs taken at various times of the area in which the school is situated can be obtained, it will be possible to identify any changes in the shape of the building that would denote its expansion. It will also be possible to compare and contrast land use around the school at different times, and possibly before it was built.

SITES AND MONUMENTS RECORDS

Information can be extracted from the local county Sites and Monuments Record (SMR). Every county has an Sites and Monuments Record usually based at a museum, at the planning office in the county or shire hall, or at the headquarters of the local archaeological unit, which you will find listed in the Archaeological Resource Book detailed in the bibliography. Each Sites and Monuments Record contains all the information that is known about all sites that have been discovered in the landscape, even though they may have since been destroyed, and all those historic places that are still in use. Each Sites and Monuments Record covers both towns and the countryside.

A Sites and Monuments Record has a series of Ordnance Survey

GEOGRAPHICAL SKILLS AND SOURCES

Bury St Edmunds: a vertical aerial photograph.

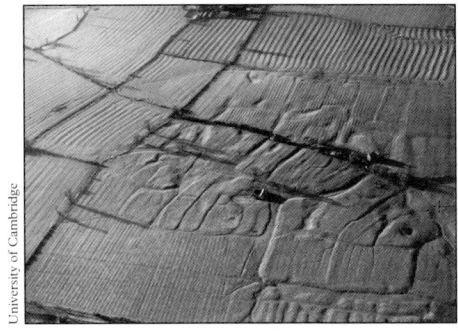

The deserted village of Olney: an oblique aerial photograph.

maps which mark each site and designate it by a unique number, often referred to as a primary record number (PRN). Sites are referenced according to the parish in which they are, or were, located. Using this number it is possible to consult files, which are often kept on computer, to extract information about that site, its plan, any photographs or slides, the finds from it, whether it has been archaeologically excavated, and any documentary evidence or published information.

Sites and Monuments Records also have a cross-referencing system that enables an enquirer to see all the known sites of a particular period. For example all the Roman sites in the county are to be seen on one map. Usually it is possible to locate all the sites with the same function, for example factories or mills. The Sites and Monuments Record is an immensely valuable and powerful tool for research at the level of the county, the parish and the individual site. Armed with this information local primary and secondary schools can undertake field visits within the area to examine the remains of places within the historic environment.

FIELDWORK SKILLS AND SOIL, GEOLOGY AND WEATHER

Each site or settlement exists among elements of the natural landscape and the influence of these elements will have had some bearing on the specific location of buildings. It will be important that children can use their knowledge of water and rivers, rocks, soils and landscape form, to discover why a particular historic feature was placed where it was and the effects of natural processes on its survival or demise and burial.

■ **Position of the site in a river valley:** where was the nearest source of water and how did it get to the site?

■ **Relief of the site and the surrounding area:** how accessible was the site? How did land relief affect the route of tracks and roads? Is there evidence that relief influenced land use?

■ **Use of local rock for building purposes:** consider why different types of rock are used for particular features, which have weathered most and what caused this weathering - frost, wind, rain, vegetation?

■ **Types of soil:** there may be various types of soil around the site; test for acidity and permeability. Would the soil have supported pastoral or arable agriculture?

■ **Influence of the weather on building position:** if a building was placed on a south-facing slope it would get more sun and longer days; living-rooms are likely to be found on the warmer, sunnier side of the building with the kitchen or industrial parts of a site having a colder aspect. The building itself could throw a shadow or affect wind direction. Wind and temperature readings could be taken at the site, to give some indication of why the particular position was chosen.

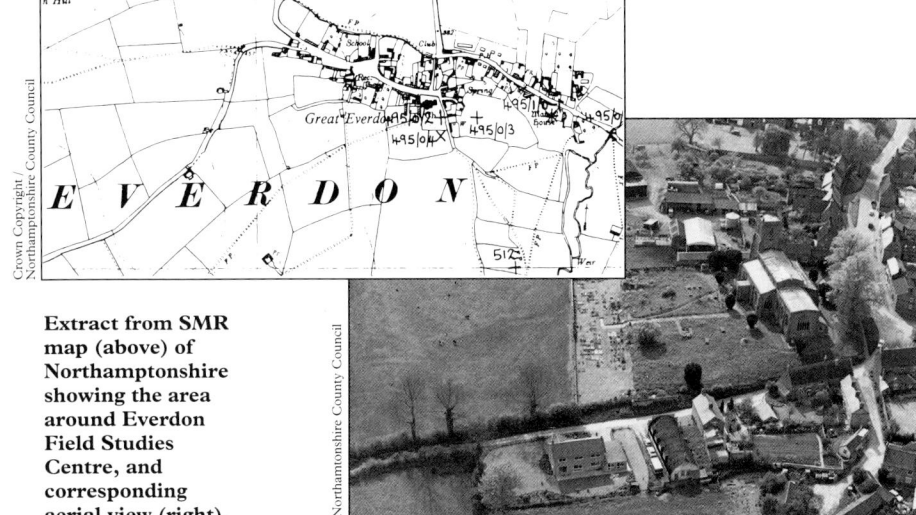

Extract from SMR map (above) of Northamptonshire showing the area around Everdon Field Studies Centre, and corresponding aerial view (right).

GEOGRAPHY AND THE HISTORIC ENVIRONMENT

SITES IN THE PRESENT LANDSCAPE

A CASE STUDY OF A RURAL AREA

The high density of historic sites of many periods is seen in a case study of just two square kilometres of countryside in West Oxfordshire. The area investigated is west of the village of Charlbury which lies in the valley of the River Evenlode thirteen miles north west of Oxford. The information for this area is found on the Oxfordshire Sites and Monuments Record, kept in the Centre for Oxfordshire Studies in Oxford's central library. Two square kilometres on the 1:50 000 Ordnance Survey map were chosen at random from a twenty-five-square-kilometre block of land around the village. They are SP 3319 and SP 3419. The landscape within these boundaries comprises a north-facing slope on clay soil which overlays oolitic limestone. It is primarily used for growing wheat, although there are small patches of woodland, and the only structures were a farm and its outbuildings which include a barn.

Over a period of three years the area was field-walked, examined from aerial photographs taken in 1948, 1963, and 1980 and documents, such as old maps and plans and books. The map shows the density of sites located. Some land was under pasture and other areas were covered by woodland, some of which was very ancient. The sites discovered in the pasture land were present as earthworks and earthworks also were located in the wooded areas. However, many sites probably remain to be discovered beneath the surface of the wood and grass.

As you can see from the plan, evidence was recovered of:

■ neolithic occupation: flint tools and arrowheads.

■ Roman settlements: pottery and a coin.

■ Saxon occupation: the burial of a warrior.

■ a medieval village which can be dated from the 12th century to its desertion in the 1400s: pottery and earthworks.

■ a medieval road: earthworks.

■ medieval fishponds: earthworks.

■ a Tudor house: still occupied as an upstanding structure.

■ a Victorian gasworks: in ruins with masonry foundations and a well still surviving.

It is likely that a track ran through the block of land that is now represented by stretches of public rights of way and a short section of tarmacked road. The main road running west was built in 1830 as part of the works associated with placing a railway station just to the north of the area.

This particular slope on the west of the River Evenlode has been a very attractive location for human beings to live. Most of the sites in the area disappeared beneath the turf some time ago. However the remains of the deserted medieval village of Walcot, which could be recognised as earthworks standing half a metre high, were only destroyed by bulldozing and ploughing in the early 1980s. At about the same time the patchwork of small fields was destroyed to make several large fields to allow the use of very large tractors and combine harvesters. With the decline of the elm tree from disease in the previous decade, what was once a sheltered place of small-scale features, is now a very exposed, windy and cold location.

A wider view of the valley of the Evenlode shows many more historic sites. There are sites surviving above ground from every period in history, including a long barrow, a hillfort and Norman castle, as well as several villages with a number of historic houses and historic wooded landscapes. The large number of sites indicates that the entire area has a long history of human occupation.

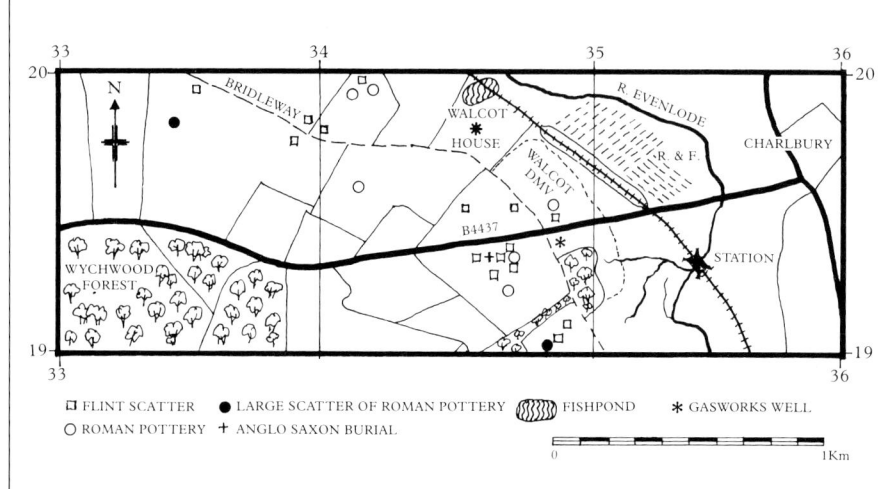

This map of a small area around Charlbury shows the continuity of occupation from the Neolithic period to the present.

SITES IN THE PRESENT LANDSCAPE

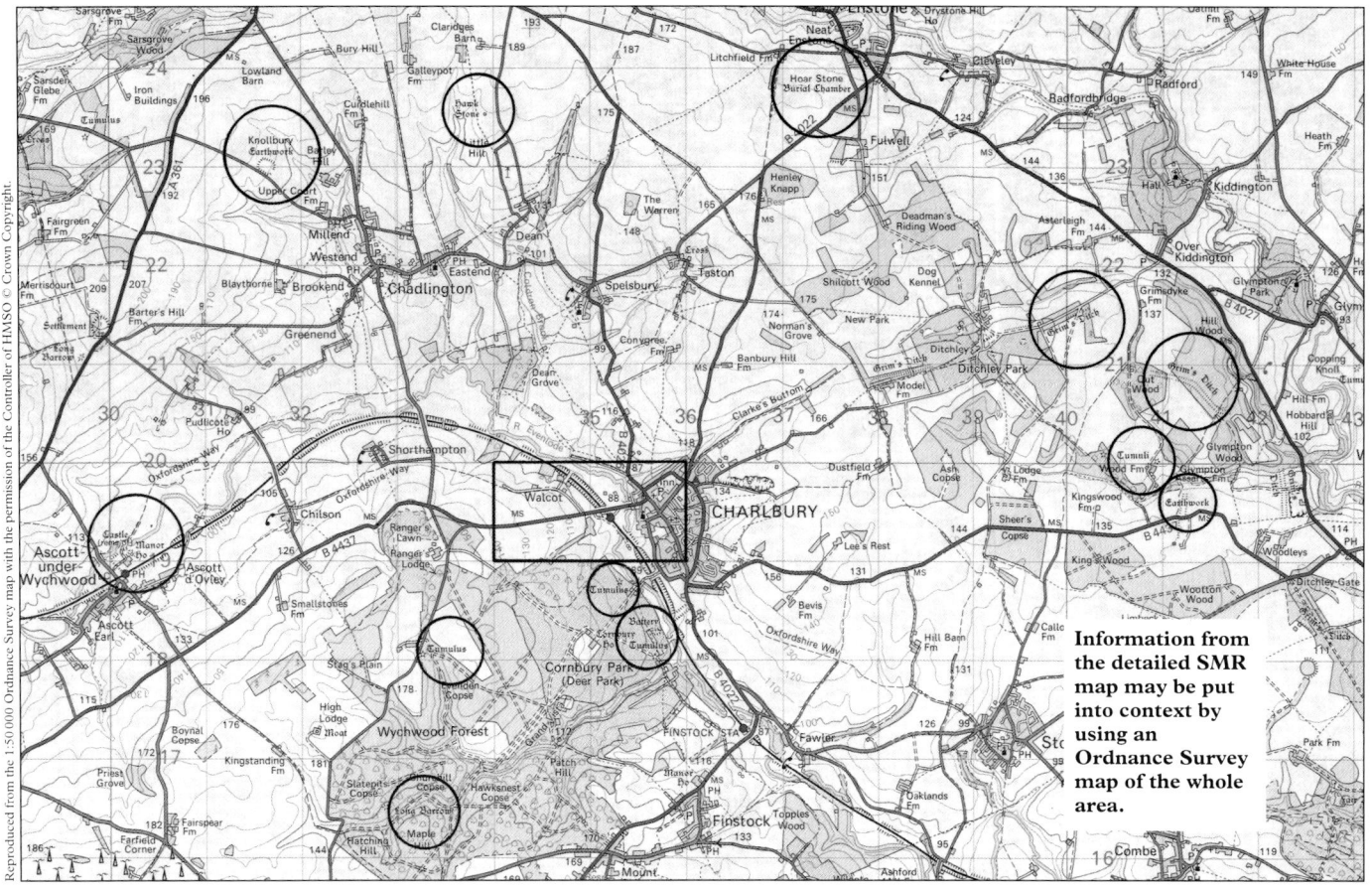

Information from the detailed SMR map may be put into context by using an Ordnance Survey map of the whole area.

ACTIVITY

Use the local Sites and Monuments Record for finding information about an area.

■ Visit your Sites and Monuments Record Office and choose an area to look at closely. The area need not be very large. It might be a few square kilometres around the school, a part of the town in which the school is located, or, in a rural district, part of the parish, or even the whole parish. You will need a large scale map (this could be a photocopy if your school or LEA has a licence to copy).

■ Decide whether you wish to look at sites of all periods or just one, for instance Roman sites. If you wish to look at sites of all periods then go straight to the map. If you wish to look at one period, it is likely that these sites have already been recorded by age, but you will have to find the appropriate Primary Record Numbers on the map.

■ Start by noting the Primary Record Numbers of the sites in the area. Look up these numbers in the catalogue and record the information on the card, or the screen if the Sites and Monuments Record has a computer database. The entry will also tell you if other plans, photographs and documents about the site are held. You will need to put the Primary Record Number on your map at the correct location.

■ When you have completed your search you will have detailed information about the sites in your area.

Using the information
■ List the sites in order of their age. Are they prehistoric, Roman, Saxon, Viking, medieval, or from a later period? You can further subdivide the prehistoric into neolithic, bronze age and iron age if you wish. You might indicate the age of the sites using a different colour ink on your map. You will be able to see the continuity of occupation of individual places by the number of sites of different ages at the same location. Later you can put all the sites of the same age on to different copies of your map. This will show you what the landscape looked like at a particular time, as far as we know.

■ Classify the sites according to their use. For example defensive sites, or ceremonial and religious places, rural buildings, industrial locations, and settlements. (There may already be a database of sites listed by function for you to use.) This would tell you whether, through time, a particular location was used for the same function. You might like to think what qualities that location had that made it so useful for a particular purpose.

■ Select sites that have more information in the shape of plans, documents and photographs for display and further study in your classroom.

GEOGRAPHY AND THE HISTORIC ENVIRONMENT

SITES AND VISITS

In this section sites have been selected that fall into defensive, religious, domestic and industrial categories so that the chosen sites will act as case studies for work on sites with similar characteristics. However, dividing sites into such categories is not clear cut. Defensive and religious sites usually have a domestic component. Agricultural sites also have a domestic aspect and often an industrial sector of some sort, and villages are likely to have had a chapel or church which was an integral part of the way they functioned. It is still useful, though, to use these categories, for they help us to sort out which aspect of a particular site was the most important. For example villages were largely agricultural in function and the church is secondary to this. A monastery however, even though it has farmland and domestic areas, is primarily a ceremonial or religious site.

WHICH SITES TO VISIT?

■ At first choose a site that is relatively well preserved, before moving on to ruins or earthworks.

■ It is helpful if a site has sufficient documentary evidence to provide material for comparison with existing features. (A guidebook or Teachers' Handbook may contain such documentary material.)

■ Ease of access to the site is essential. In the process of an enquiry it may be necessary to revisit the site to clarify points and identify further questions.

The majority of the sites described here are cared for by English Heritage. Although a small number of sites is described, in most of the categories there will be a number of similar sites in different parts of the country.

In this section the emphasis is on fieldwork. Geographical questions that focus on the past use of a site prompt activities that could be used as fieldwork tasks. Not all the questions can be answered at each site perhaps because the evidence no longer exists or has not been discovered yet. It is important that children are aware of this limitation of evidence. It might lead to hypothesising from the evidence that is available, although

children should begin to understand the problems of bias that may arise from the use of incomplete evidence. With the experience of working on a well-preserved monument behind them, the children can then examine local sites which had a similar function and compare and contrast their findings with the exemplar site.

GEOGRAPHY AND THE HISTORIC ENVIRONMENT

DEFENSIVE SITES

The term defensive has been chosen because not all the sites discussed had a purely military role or were concerned with attack. All, however, were concerned with the protection of land or people. Their roles and the area they were defending varied and this is directly related to the section of the population that they were built to defend. Defensive sites have survived to the present day because of the massiveness of their structures, which were built to withstand aggression and therefore had to be of substantial construction. The variety of forms reflects the development of the technology of attack and defence.

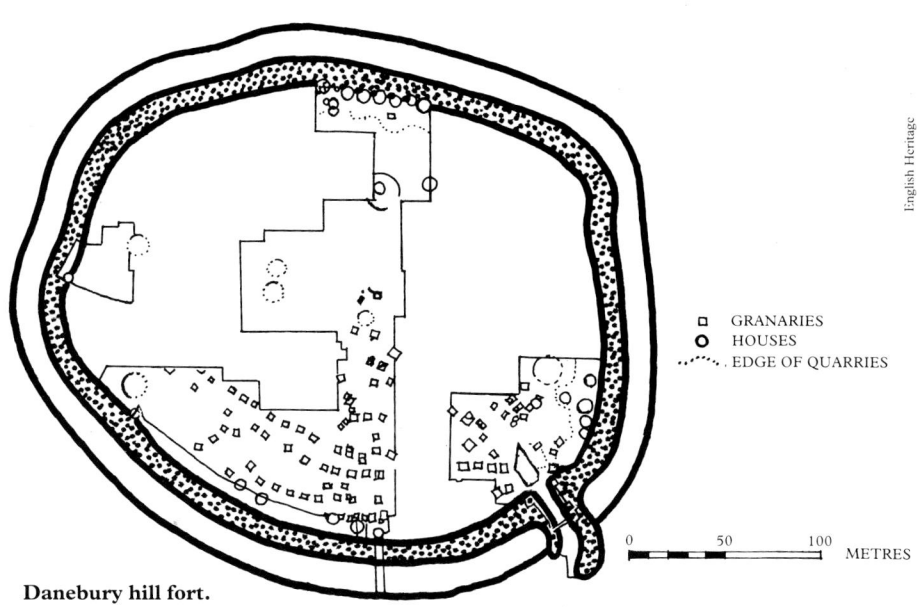

Danebury hill fort.

HILL FORTS

Danebury, Hampshire
(Map reference: SU 323376)

Most hill forts are a product of the iron age and they survived until the Roman Conquest in the years following AD43, some also being reoccupied in the post Roman period. Built of earth and wood, the defences ring a hilltop.

At Danebury the hill fort is situated on the end of an east-west ridge at 143 metres above sea-level. Three distinct defensive circuits can be seen. The inner earthwork, the earliest, encloses a roughly circular area. Originally it had two entrances, the east entrance and a south-west entrance which was blocked up sometime during the iron age. Between the earthworks of the two entrances on the south side of the fort runs another bank and ditch, whilst enclosing everything is an outer earthwork. The gateways were remodelled several times during the use of the fort.

Unfortunately the interiors of hill forts are rarely available for study as they have all too often been destroyed by later use, particularly ploughing. At Danebury,

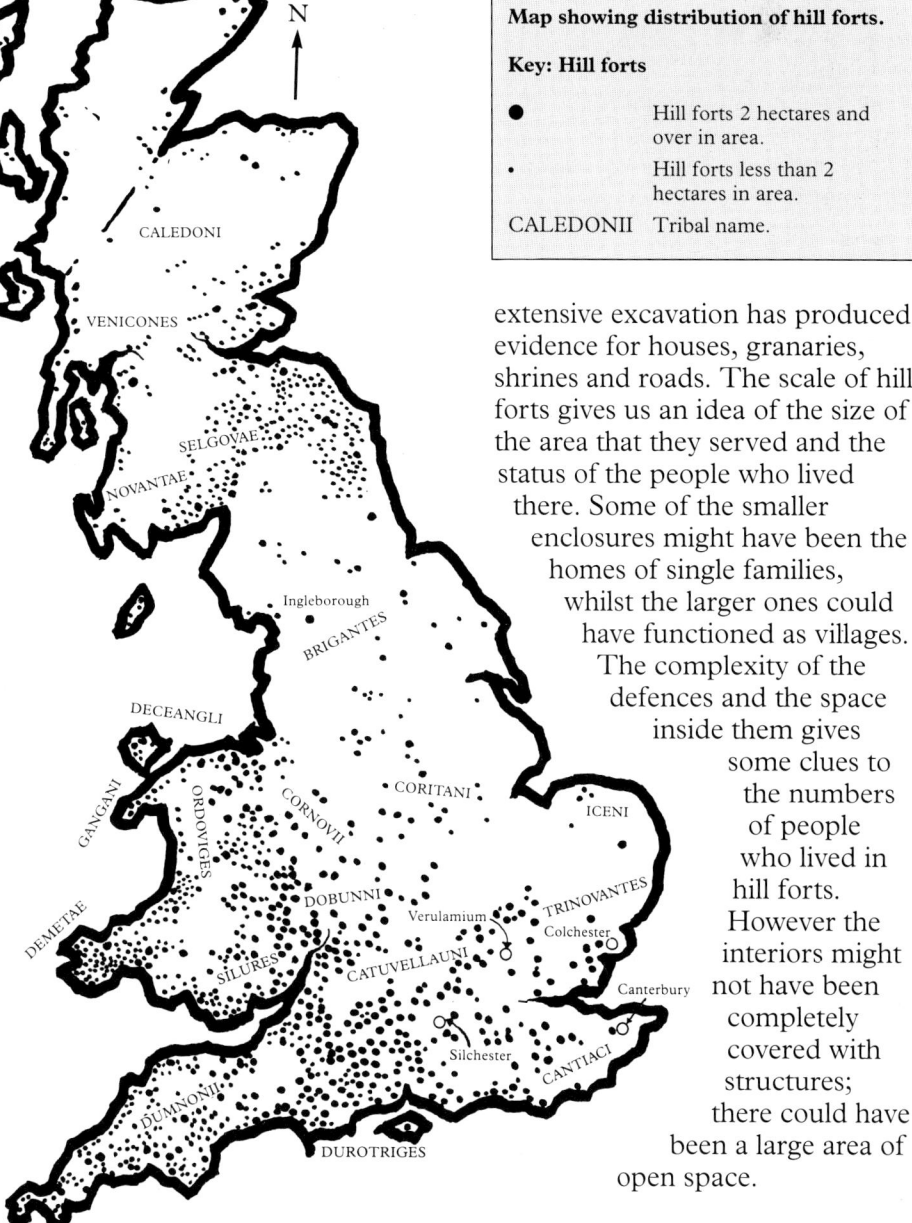

extensive excavation has produced evidence for houses, granaries, shrines and roads. The scale of hill forts gives us an idea of the size of the area that they served and the status of the people who lived there. Some of the smaller enclosures might have been the homes of single families, whilst the larger ones could have functioned as villages. The complexity of the defences and the space inside them gives some clues to the numbers of people who lived in hill forts. However the interiors might not have been completely covered with structures; there could have been a large area of open space.

13

DEFENSIVE SITES

Although hill forts seem to have been focal points in the landscape, the relationship to and the size of the district on which they would be able to draw to maintain their inhabitants is usually unknown. It is possible that besides being permanent settlements they also might have acted as refuges in times of social or inter-tribal unrest, and as markets or trade and administrative centres. Excavation has indicated that very few industrial activities actually took place within the ramparts and that the hillfort was a major market for goods being produced outside the fort, often at some distance. These goods included pottery and metal-work. In the immediate area of Danebury, aerial photographs show fields, trackways and enclosures.

ROMAN FORTS

Housesteads (Vercovicium) Northumberland
(Map reference: NY 790687)
We know a great deal about Roman forts from excavation and documentary evidence of the Roman Empire. Roman forts were military garrisons, strategically sited and part of a national network. They existed as strong points in the landscape to protect the detachment of soldiers who ensured that the conquered peoples in the surrounding area did not threaten the rest of the province of *Britannia*. The forts also may have been sited to protect sources of raw materials and strategic crossing points of rivers. They were sometimes located close to important native iron age centres to oversee them.

A ditch and a rampart would enclose a playing card shaped space in which a unit of between 200 and 400 men were accommodated. A formal pattern of roads within the fort divided it up into areas which contained buildings with specific functions. The soldiers' barracks were at the front, *praetentura*, and at the back, *retentura*, of the fort to facilitate access to the fighting platform if the need arose. The bath buildings at Housesteads were outside the fort to reduce danger from fire and to capitalise on the Knag Burn, a stream running 100 metres east of the fort. Outside the fort was a *vicus* where local inhabitants traded with the garrison. There was also a parade-ground, and terraces, for the garrison grew its own crops. Often the fort grew and shrank in size depending on the size of the garrison and this is reflected in the shape of the surviving earthworks of its defences.

Vercovicium was part of the defensive system of Hadrian's Wall. Along the wall are placed forts. Between each fort are milecastles, and between each milecastle are turrets. A road ran immediately

Map showing distribution of Roman forts linked by roads.

Housesteads Roman fort.

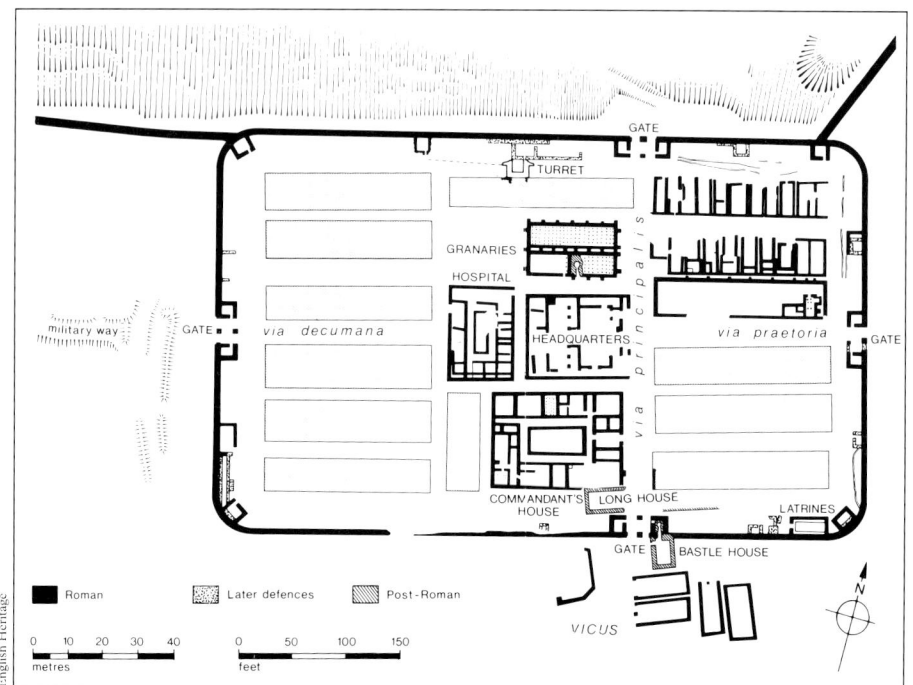

DEFENSIVE SITES

behind the wall where the terrain allowed and the whole military area was sealed off by the *vallum* or ditch.

Forts were often positioned a day's march from the next fort along the road, thereby offering the opportunity of support if attacked. There was likely to be a signal system, perhaps on a nearby hilltop, to ensure rapid communication of messages. Although the forts we visit today lie in the upland areas of Britain, this gives a rather false picture reflecting the final stages of the Roman occupation. Forts would have been built throughout southern Britain during the early phases of the conquest. As these areas became settled, the military presence moved to the advancing frontier and the earlier forts were demolished. Since they were made of turf and timber they have left little evidence of their existence and frequently new towns were constructed over their site, as, for example at Wroxeter in Shropshire. The forts in the highland areas generally had a long life and therefore many were rebuilt in stone, and so the evidence for their presence tends to survive.

CASTLES

Beeston Castle, Cheshire
(Map reference: SJ 537593)
Castles came to England with the Norman Conquest, techniques having been particularly developed in Normandy during the period prior to the invasion. Castles reflected the practice of feudalism with its hierarchical structure. Castles were built to defend the person and the lands of one man: the lord, who might be the king or a baron or knight. Beeston was a baronial castle and later a royal one. The castle acted as a base for the patrolling of the lord's lands by knights. If the lordship was a particularly big one there might be several important castles sited at key points in the area. Castles like Rochester were built to guard important river crossings, Orford was sited to control the mouth of the Dunwich river, Dover to ensure the safety of a major seaport. Castles on the Welsh and Scottish borders, such as Beeston, were placed to stop raiders crossing into the realm of England. Some castles were placed in towns to act as administrative centres and therefore had to be accessible to the population, although they were distinct from the town and had separate defences. Castles held by important clerics, archbishops and bishops, were frequently sited near their cathedral churches, Durham being a fine example.

The choice of a specific site for the fortress was dependent on defensibility. A rocky outcrop, such as Beeston, provided maximum defensibility, keeping the short-range weapons of the day at a distance. Sometimes a river spur or stretch of high ground was used and wide and deep ditches were dug to make the site more difficult to attack. Often the castle seems to be over-large, as at Beeston, with a small keep

ACTIVITY

Making a section through defences

When we look at a section of something, we are taking a slice out of it and looking at its vertical shape. A section tells us more about how the defences worked. It shows us the obstacles to the attacker as the attacker would have seen them as he looked up. It also shows us what the defender would have seen as they looked down. A section can also give us clues to what sort of tactics and weapons were used. For example, lots of ditches shows us that the attackers would be expected to be on foot, whilst very thick walls indicates the defence was against stone throwers, cannon or guns.

■ To draw a section it is useful to have a scale of some sort. A human scale will do, such as a child, or a teacher.

■ Start at the lowest point outside the site and sketch in the slope of the defences using the figure as the measurement unit. If the defences are vertical get the figure to stand at the base of the wall.

■ Estimate the shape and width of the top of the defences.

■ Sketch the slope of the rear of the defences again using the figure as the measurement unit.

■ Shade in the solid areas black and add a rough scale, the place and date.

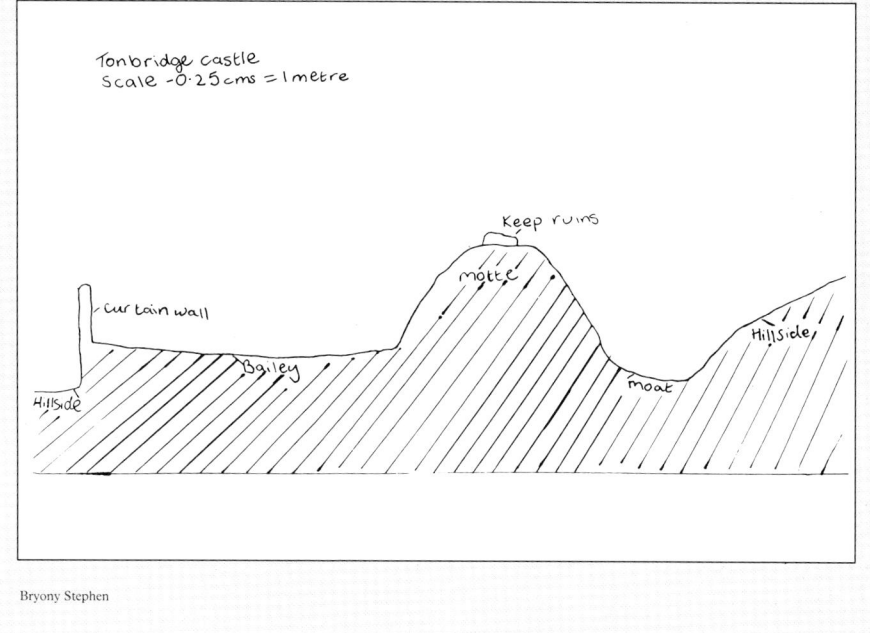

Bryony Stephen

DEFENSIVE SITES

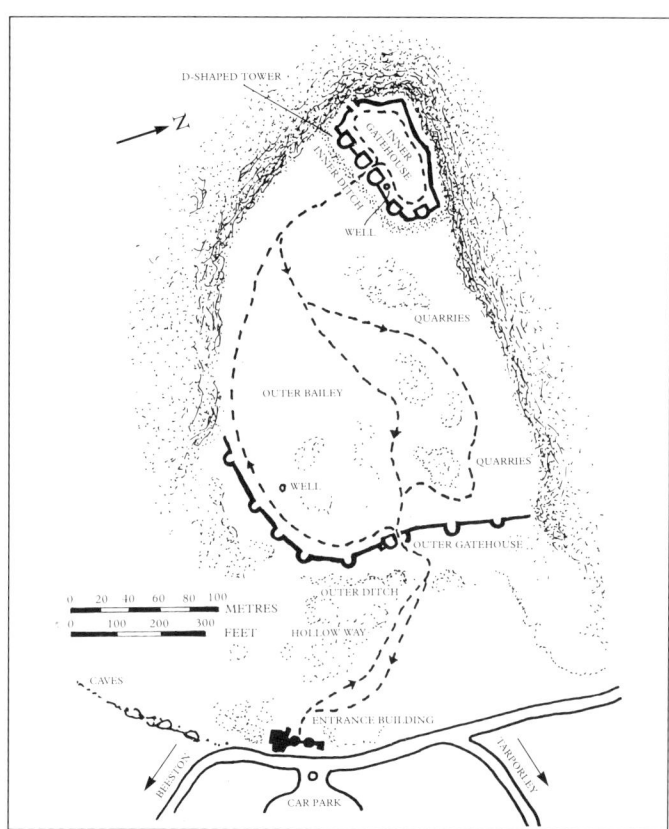

Beeston Castle: Reconstruction drawing (above) of Beeston Castle in 1265.
As can be seen from the plan (right), the castle walls had to enclose a large area to ensure safety from attack.

and extensive walls enclosing a relatively vast area. This was necessitated by the castle having to command the whole of the high ground to ensure that it could not be used by an attacker. The most feared form of attack was through the mining of stone-built defences. Where feasible, castles were sited on rock, like Beeston, to make such an attack impossible.

The majority of castles were sited in flatter terrain without the benefit of a natural feature to protect them. The design of the fortress had to compensate for the lack of natural defences resulting in high walls and towers, well-protected gateways, water filled moats and the gradual addition of further circuits of walls as the range of artillery weapons lengthened.

Castles developed from simple motte and bailey structures to extensive stone-built complexes that answered a variety of needs of the lord and his retinue. Initially the defensive properties of the castle would have been paramount, but as the country became more settled the personal luxury of the lord became the dominating factor in a land becoming increasingly more unified.

PILLBOXES

Kimmeridge, Dorset
(Map reference: SY 855803)
Many schools in coastal and some inland areas have a Second World War pillbox near them as these were built as coastal and inland lines of defence. They were relatively simple structures built of reinforced concrete with gun loops facing the direction of invasion and were intended for the use of rifles, machine-guns and anti-tank rifles. They defended the coastal strip along with lines of concrete tank defences and barbed wire. Inland they were sited on rivers, alongside railway lines and canals to offer lines of defence if the enemy forces managed to breach the coastal defences. Sometimes they were obvious in the landscape, but frequently they were camouflaged as everyday structures. They were part of a national strategy and built very rapidly, causing a national crisis in stocks of cement.

Pillbox at Kimmeridge.

Pillboxes from the Second World War.

16

DEFENSIVE SITES

LINES OF ENQUIRY

What was this place like? Using a map or making fieldwork sketches:

Find the highest point in the place.

- Observe and examine the landscape around the defended site.

- Using a map, determine how far you can see and whether the visibility is better on any one side.

- Find a method of measuring which side is the most exposed to the wind.

- Look for natural features that you think make this site a strong or weak one.

Walk around the defences.

- Outline the defences on a map noting where there are differences, for example where there is an increased number of lines of ramparts, or where the ramparts are higher or lower.

- Locate the gateways and map them. If possible walk, or map, the routes from the outside to the centre of the defended area and identify how it is defended and by what sort of features.

- Locate and map the towers on the ramparts and find how they relate to each other and to the walls – whether they are in front or behind them and how far apart they are. From this information, consider what sort of weapons might have been in use and their likely range.

Explore inside the defences.

- Search for any obvious sources of water inside the fort and any evidence that might suggest past supplies of water. If there are no such indications, determine where the nearest supply is, and its distance and direction.

- Examine and make a sketch plan of any structures or their traces. Consider what their function might have been, why they are in a particular position and how they were connected to each other.

- Enquire if any artefacts have been found inside the fort, find out where they were found and consider what information they might give about the activities that took place inside the defences.

Why was this place like it was, how and why did it differ from, or resemble other places? Using the data gathered above try to answer a series of questions:

- Why was this site chosen?

- How did its defences work?

- What relationship is there between the shape of the defences and the terrain?

- Why were the buildings inside it located where they were?

- What were they used for? Who was this fort built to defend?

Using reference books and maps or experience of other sites.

- How does this fort compare with others like it in size and shape?

- How does it compare with defensive sites of other times?

- Does it have the same sort of siting?

- Are its internal buildings and their siting similar to others?

In what ways was this place connected to other places? Using fieldwork evidence and maps:

- Is there evidence for agricultural settlement outside the fort?

- Is there a town near? What relationship does the fort have to this settlement?

- Look for evidence of roads linking the fort to other forts or other places.

- How many other forts can you see or find on the map? Are they bigger or smaller than the site you are on? Do you think they might have been in the territory of the largest fort?

- What transport might have been used? What materials might have been transported to and from the fort?

How has this place changed and why? Using the site, the guidebook, and maps:

- Try to locate evidence in the form of structures or alterations to structures that might indicate either growth or shrinkage of the site.

- Look for evidence of destruction or disuse of the site and try to explain it.

- Think about the present use of the site compared to its previous usage. How has this change of use affected the remaining structures?

What would it have felt like to be in this place?

The information collected should allow the children to gain an impression of what it might have been like to live in the place when it was in use at a particular time.

- Suggest what might have been happening at a particular location within the site at a particular time of the day or year.

- Think about which part of the site was the busiest and noisiest, and which part emptiest and quietest.

Information gained from further work in the classroom will add to the children's impressions of the sites, particularly details of the attitudes, values and beliefs of its inhabitants.

GEOGRAPHY AND THE HISTORIC ENVIRONMENT

CEREMONIAL AND RELIGIOUS SITES

There are common spatial elements in both ceremonial and religious sites. There tends to be a linear feature such as a ditch or a wall that delimits the sacred area from the surrounding landscape. There is usually evidence that offers an indication of possible processional routes within that sacred area. The focal point of the ceremonies that took place at a location can often be identified.

PREHISTORIC CEREMONIAL SITES

Avebury, Wiltshire
(Centred on map reference: SU 103700)

During the later neolithic period, about 2,600 BC, the Avebury area formed a large ceremonial landscape whose elements comprised the Avebury Stone Circles, or Henge, the Avenue that joined them to the Sanctuary, Silbury Hill, Windmill Hill and the surrounding long barrows. Whilst it is impossible to be sure, it would appear that the Avebury Henge, the Sanctuary and the linking Avenue form the core of the complex.

The Avebury Henge (SU 103700) comprises the Great Circle which was made up of 98 upright stones, and within this, two smaller circles, now known as the North and South Circles. The stones were sarsens, a form of local sandstone resting on the surrounding chalk surface. It appears that the likely focus of any ceremonies that might have been carried out at the site was within these two circles either at the now-vanished Obelisk Stone within the southern circle, or at the Cove, three massive sarsen stones forming a three-sided enclosure, within the northern circle.

The West Kennet Avenue (SU 105695) leads away from the south entrance of the Great Circle

Plan of Avebury.

Aerial view of Avebury.

in a south-easterly direction towards the Sanctuary. It was formed of about a hundred sets of paired stones and it appears to have been a processional route. The Sanctuary (SU 118679) at the eastern end of the Avenue, was in use as a series of concentric wooden circles, some possibly supporting a roof, before they were replaced, or enclosed, by two concentric circles of sarsen stones.

Many of the stones of the circles and the Avenue have been destroyed and used for roadmaking or buildings, but the remainder form a very impressive monument inside the silted up ditch. The Sanctuary was totally destroyed in the eighteenth century, and the positions of its posts were recovered by excavation. They are now marked by concrete plinths

The circles are frequently described as being a ceremonial centre linked to birth, death and regeneration. The Sanctuary was possibly the site of a timber building for social and religious gatherings. The Avenue is seen as a processional route from the Henge to the Sanctuary.

In the area immediately around the Avebury monuments are the even more enigmatic sites of Silbury Hill and Windmill Hill. Silbury Hill (SU 100685) is the largest man made prehistoric mound in Europe. It lies 1.5 kilometres south of the Avebury Henge, and is of approximately the same date.

CEREMONIAL AND RELIGIOUS SITES

Windmill Hill (SU 086714) is a causewayed enclosure on a hill top 2 kilometres north-west of the Henge. It is thought that it is earlier than both the Henge and Silbury Hill, that is from 3,700 to 2,500 BC. Causeway enclosures are usually seen as being places of refuge, where the exposure of the dead was carried out prior to burial, or the site of tribal gatherings.

There are more than twenty long barrows, repositories for bones rather than for complete bodies, within a three-mile radius of Avebury. It seems that the area was held in some awe by the prehistoric builders of these monuments. The scale of the individual sites indicates their importance to the contemporary society.

CHURCHES

St Mary's Church Fairford, Gloucestershire
(Map reference SP 151011)

There are more than 18,000 churches in England and each church, whether at the heart of a village or an urban parish, has its own geography of symbolism and ritual.

St Mary's is aligned east-west, and is in the shape of a cross with its side chapels being the horizontal axis. It had its areas for the worshippers and those for the celebrant of the holy rites and his assistants. The chancel, where Mass was said daily, was the focus of the worship. It was railed off from the nave to ensure that the congregation did not cross into the sacred area. On the south side of the chancel was the lavabo where the holy vessels were washed and on the same side were the sedilia where the priest and his servers sat.

Within the nave there are signs of social geography in the placing of the local dignitarys' pews, which are often decorated and, in some churches, enclosed. The prosperity of the wool trade in the fourteenth century caused the parish to become richer, so aisles were added and chapels were set up in the transepts. Here Mass was said for the souls of the benefactors.

The churchyard developed on the south side, presumably along the main pathway to the south door, the main entrance to the church. Also outside the south door was a preaching cross. It was here that trading often took place.

Churches had to be accessible to their users, so their location in relation to streets and the position of their doors tells us a great deal about the layout, both topographical and social, of the towns and villages which supported them. St Mary's lies near the wide market-place, and this indicates that the market probably developed outside the church door and in the churchyard.

St Mary's lies on a low terrace above the flood plain of the River Thames. The selection of its site was controlled by the influence of the terrain, tradition and the distribution of population. Any area susceptible to flooding was ruled out and the underlying geology needed to have considerable weight-bearing qualities. The clay of the flood plain would not support the weight of a stone church. There needed also to be a supply of water to use in rituals, and enough room for a graveyard. Tradition, such as the presence of a pre-Christian religious site might also influence the siting of the church.

The high quality of the Cotswold stone of St Mary's allowed masons of all periods to produce refined decorative work for pinnacles and statues, and its windows are large and ornate. Its tall parapetted stone tower also indicates that this was a district where good building stone for the quoins that form the corners of square towers was available. In Norfolk and Suffolk, where local stone is poor, round towers are common. In the same area flint is used as a wall facing with stone window and door tracery.

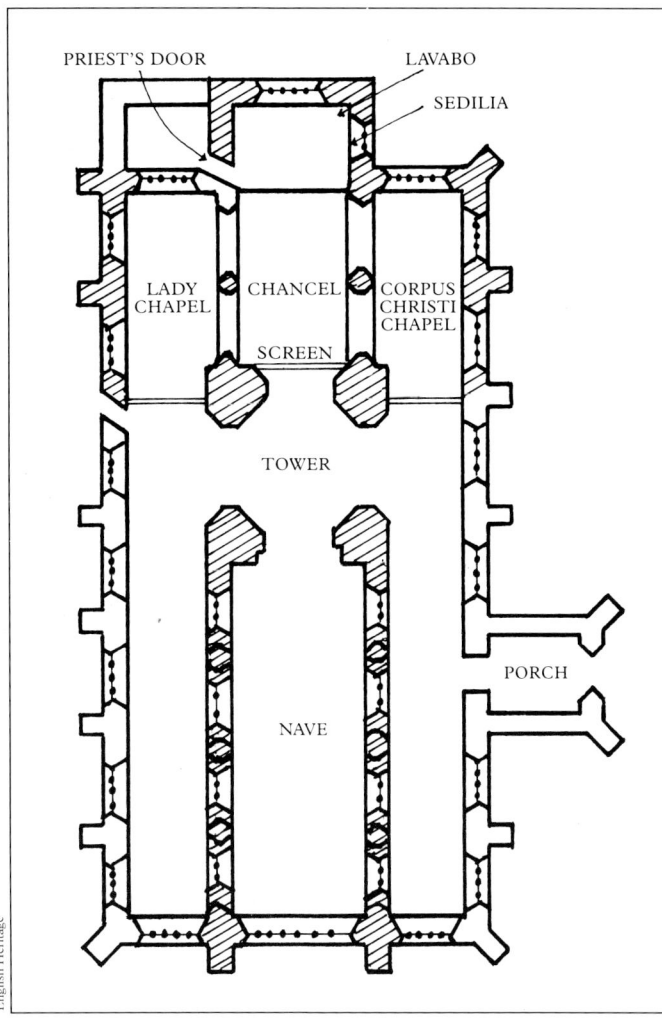

St Mary's Church. The plan shows the main phases of building.

CEREMONIAL AND RELIGIOUS SITES

Aerial view of Rievaulx Abbey.

Reconstruction drawing of Rievaulx Abbey.

ABBEYS

Rievaulx Abbey, North Yorkshire
(Map reference: SE 577849)

Abbeys and priories existed in towns and in the countryside. Some were in secluded places to enable the inhabitants to avoid the distraction of the secular world. Although the shape and main function of abbeys and priories were similar, their members would have belonged to different religious orders whose rules would have directed the monks and nuns to different tasks: caring for the sick, running schools and almshouses, and praying.

Rievaulx Abbey was the first foundation of the Cistercian Order in Yorkshire. The order had been instituted in 1098 at Citeaux in Burgundy, in an attempt to recapture the high ideals of earlier communities. The monks were committed to leading a simple life, eating plain food and filling the time not spent in prayer with manual labour. Their habit was made of unbleached, undyed wool, leading to the name 'white monks'.

Each area of the abbey had its own specific function. The dormitory or dorter had its night stairs to allow direct access to the church for night services. The latrine block or reredorter was directly accessible from the dormitory - for obvious reasons. The cloister is where monks studied, copied manuscripts or took moderate exercise. The infirmary's main function was for the care of the elderly, although it was also used for the sick. Here strict rules about diet were sometimes relaxed. The chapter house was used for meetings and for conducting day-to-day business. The layout at Rievaulx reflected the communal approach to monastic life. This is in direct contrast to monasteries of the Carthusian order, such as Mount Grace Priory, whose members lived an almost completely solitary life in separate cells, rarely meeting even in church.

The main focus of an abbey was its church. This was usually built on an east-west line with the altar at the east end facing the Holy Land and catching the early light for the celebration of Mass. However at Rievaulx the limitations of the valley were such that the church was built on a north-south line. The Cistercian community at Rievaulx was divided into the literate choir monks, who said Mass, and the lay brothers. These lay brothers, who were illiterate, were often skilled workers: masons, carpenters, dairymen or shepherds. Their role in the abbey was that of practical support.

The layout of the abbey at Rievaulx, and of any abbey with a community of lay brothers, reflected this division. At Rievaulx the lay brothers were housed in the West Range, where they had their own dormitory, reredorter and refectory. The church would have been divided with a rood screen to separate the eastern end of the nave - for choir monks - from the western end - for lay brothers.

Water supply was an important element in the siting and building of any abbey or priory. The reredorter or latrine would have been built over an existing stream or over an artificial channel constructed for that purpose. A clean water supply was necessary both for the laver, or washing trough, and for the kitchens, which were always sited upstream of the reredorters!

Rievaulx, like several other Yorkshire abbeys, became prosperous through the wool trade. Evidence of this prosperity, and a dilution of earlier austere ideals, can be seen in the rebuilding and extension of the abbey church in around 1200.

No monasteries escaped the dissolution in the sixteenth century, when all abbey and priory sites were sold off. Many monastic buildings were almost totally destroyed. Some abbeys survived as cathedrals, while some abbey churches became parish churches. Other monastic buildings were converted into mansions for the aristocracy, while some were used as farmhouses or out buildings. Materials were often reused for local building work.

CEREMONIAL AND RELIGIOUS SITES

LINES OF ENQUIRY

What was this place like? Using a map or making fieldwork sketches:

General site:
■ Describe and map the location of the place of worship in relation to the physical landscape, the nearest settlement or part of a large settlement.

Inside the place of worship:
■ Make a plan of the structure noting the different areas such as nave and chancel.
■ Locate on the plan any prominent features, particularly altars and any evidence that the church was divided into sections.
■ Add to your plan the furniture used by the priest and congregation. Do the pews show any sign that they might be reserved for those of high rank?
■ Use a compass to find the direction of the axes of the different parts of the building.
■ Find the main access routes for the priest and the congregation and add these to the plan. Examine the wear patterns on the floor to ascertain the routes taken by those who use the church.

Outside the place of worship:
If you are studying a parish church:
■ Examine the graveyard and decide where its boundaries are, what shape it is and on which side of the church it is widest.
■ Locate the highest and lowest part of the graveyard.
■ Make a sketch plan of the gates and pathways in the graveyard and any other features such as a preaching cross.
■ Try to work out in which direction the graveyard developed by looking at the dates on the gravestones. See if you can find any evidence for occupations in the past by examining the inscriptions on the stones.

If you are studying a monastic site:
■ Are there any signs that the buildings were used by a community of lay brothers as well as choir monks? Mark these areas onto your plan of the church.
■ Locate in the church the day and night stairs for the choir monks and the lay brothers. Follow these routes to find the dormitories of the monks and brothers and the cloister.
■ Draw a sketch plan of the cloister and the rooms off it noting their functions, chapter house, refectory etc.
■ Locate the infirmary, the reredorters and the abbot's house, and mark them onto your plan of the abbey.
■ Outside the cloister area look for any evidence of agricultural or industrial activity.
■ Find the nearest source of water and plot how it was channelled through the monastic buildings, and its direction of flow. Notice the relative positions of the kitchens and reredorters or latrines.

Why was this place as it was? How and why did it differ from, or resemble other places? Using the data gathered above try to answer a series of questions:

■ Why was the place built in this shape?
■ Why was it sited here?
■ How did people get access to it?
■ How did the graveyard develop?
■ Which routes would they have used to move around the structure?
■ Which is the most sacred part of the structure and what evidence is there to show how it was used?

For monastic buildings
■ Which parts of the monastery were used at particular times of the day according to the rule?
■ How would the monks have moved around the monastery and when? What industrial and agricultural activities took place and where were they carried out?

Using reference books and maps or experience of other sites:

■ How does this church compare with others like it in shape and size? How does it compare with other churches of different or similar date? Does it have the same sort of siting?
■ How are the abbey buildings similar or different to others of the same order or different orders? Why is this?

In what ways was this place connected to other places? Using fieldwork evidence and maps:

■ Find the house where the parish clergy lived and the tithe barn.
■ Find the parish boundaries and the churches of the surrounding parishes.
■ Is the church connected to a castle or country house? Was the church on a pilgrims' route and if so where were they going and why?

For monastic sites:
■ Did the monastery have any granges or outlying properties and if so where and how far and in what direction where they?
■ Did the monastery have any daughter house and if so where? Find other sites of the same order or different orders.

How has this place changed and why? Using fieldwork and guidebooks:

■ Can you find any evidence in the use of different building and architectural styles, the blocking of windows and doors, or the abandonment of aisles that indicates that this structure expanded or contracted. Why do you think this might have been so?
■ Is there any evidence for the changing of styles of worship?

What would it have felt like to be in this place?

The information collected should allow the children to gain an impression of what it might have been like to live in the place when it was in use at a particular time.
■ Suggest what might have been happening at a particular location within the site at a particular time of the day or year.
Information gained from further work in the classroom will add to the children's impressions of the sites, particularly details of the attitudes, values and beliefs of their inhabitants.

GEOGRAPHY AND THE HISTORIC ENVIRONMENT

INDUSTRIAL SITES

The factors of location, accessibility of raw materials and skills, the manufacturing process and the marketing of the product are the key issues in studying industrial sites.

PREHISTORIC INDUSTRIAL SITES

Grimes Graves, Norfolk
(Map reference: TL 818898)

Grimes Graves is a neolithic flint mine in south-west Norfolk. Between 700 and 800 shafts and shallow pits were dug over an area of 34 acres to gain access to 'floorstone', high quality flint that was used to make tools and weapons. Depending on the depth at which the 'floorstone' could be found, it was either open-cast mined, or retrieved by the digging of shallow pits up to 14 feet below the surface and bell-shaped so that the maximum amount of flint could be extracted. Shafts, some as much as 40ft deep, were sunk where the flint was at a greater depth, with the overburden of sand and boulder clay being removed, possibly with wooden shovels, and the harder chalk being prised out with red deer antler picks. Waste and the mined flint were probably removed using skin bags hauled from the surface. The miners reached the bottom of the shaft using some sort of fibre rope. At the level of the flint seam small galleries were cut radiating in all directions from the main shaft. It has been suggested that three miners could have dug and removed all the flint from a mine in about six months, and that all the pits could have been dug in about three hundred years.

At the surface the flint was knapped into roughly shaped axes on site at one of the dozens of flint knapping floors that have been

Reconstruction of Grimes Graves.

Aerial views of Grimes Graves. The depressions, surrounded by waste material produced during mining can clearly be seen from the air.

INDUSTRIAL SITES

LINES OF ENQUIRY

What was this place like? Using a map or making fieldwork sketches:

Outside the main manufacturing area:

■ Examine the physical location of the industrial site to locate raw materials, or sources of power, or the storage of those sources.

■ Look for signs of a transportation system in the shape of roads or tracks, stables, quays on rivers or canals, or railway loading bays.

■ Can you find evidence of waste products on or near the site?

Inside the main manufacturing area:

■ Look for evidence of machinery in the form of engines, or motors or water-wheels.

■ Examine the buildings for clues of the sort of process that might have taken place there, particularly those connected with the making of tools.

■ Find out how the source of energy reached the individual parts of the site and how the product was moved into and around the site during manufacture.

■ Look for evidence of storage of the finished product and its route out of the site.

■ Look for the offices of the works and any form of weighing of raw or finished materials.

Why was this place as it was? How and why did it differ from, or resemble other places?

Using the data gathered above try to answer a series of questions:

■ Why was this site chosen? Which factors determined the site's location? If there are no obvious physical reasons could it have been for skills already in the area?

■ What makes it an industrial site? How did the manufacturing process work and which buildings did it use and in what order? Can you draw a plan or network of the manufacturing process?

■ How similar or different is it to other industrial sites of earlier or later periods that you have seen? What evidence is there that a particular product was made here?

Using reference books and maps or experience of other sites:

■ How does this industrial site compare with others used for the same purpose in size, shape and organisation? How does it differ from other sites making different products?

■ How does its siting differ from those other sites?

■ How does it compare with industrial sites that were in operation earlier or later?

In what ways was this place connected to other places? Using fieldwork, museums, documentary evidence or maps:

■ Locate where the raw materials came from, how they were transported and where the finished product was sent to. Plot this information onto a map.

■ Use the same sources to find where the workforce lived.

■ Find where other sites used for a similar purpose were located and decide whether this area was a centre for the industry and why this might have been so.

How has this place changed and why? Using fieldwork and guidebooks:

■ Can you find any evidence for the growth or contraction of the site?

■ Try to find clues that the source of energy for making the product changed during its lifetime, or that the manufacturing process changed.

■ Find out why the place stopped working and look for clues in the structures that tell of the results of its closure. Has the structure been put to new use?

What would it have felt like to be in this place?

The information collected should allow the children to gain an impression of what it might have been like to live in the place when it was in use at a particular time.

■ Think about what you would have seen and felt at a particular part of the site.

■ Suggest what might have been happening at a particular location within the site at a particular time of the day or year.

Information gained from further work in the classroom will add to the children's impressions of the sites, particularly details of the attitudes, values and beliefs of their inhabitants.

---

found, and which are surrounded by waste flint flakes up to five feet thick. The floors were either on the heath close to the pits or in the top of partly infilled pits, which would have given some protection from the elements for there is no evidence of huts at the site. The problem of waste chalk was sometimes solved by filling in galleries that had been cleared of flint already, thereby saving a considerable amount of work.

Before these mines were opened axes had been made from high-quality flint found on the surface or finished axes had been brought to East Anglia from Cornwall and the Lake District. It is not known if a large export trade developed from Grimes Graves or where the finishing of the axes was completed.

INDUSTRIAL SITES

SITES OF THE INDUSTRIAL REVOLUTION

Stott Park Bobbin Mill, Cumbria
(Map reference: SD 373883)

Bobbins and reels were used in the Lancashire cotton mills and were the objects on which the cotton was wound during the spinning process. The bobbin-making industry grew up in the Lake District because of its proximity to the mills, its profusion of coppice woodlands and the reservoir of woodworking skills that was found there. Coppicing involved the cutting of the trees, specifically birch and ash, to create the growth of many long poles from each tree stump. Originally the bobbins were made in several pieces and then glued together. However by the middle of the nineteenth century machinery allowed the production of one-piece bobbins.

At Stott Park Bobbin Mill the process of producing the bobbins is clearly seen in the function of the surviving buildings. The wood arrived in cartloads of a ton a time and was either stored in the coppice barns or cut by circular saw outside the mill into suitable lengths, which were then piled in stacks of different sizes. Next the pieces of wood were bored with a hole through the centre and placed on a roughing lathe which cut the wood into the approximate shape. The wood was cut when wet but easier to finish when dry, so before the product was finished it was placed in a drying shed, and the central hole was cleaned out. Then the bobbins were turned on a finishing lathe and shaped by various cutting tools into the desired pattern and finally polished by being rotated in a revolving drum which contained a lump of paraffin wax. To turn the machinery which sculpted the bobbins out of the coppice poles, the power of the Lakeland streams was used, although the waterwheel, installed in 1858 and producing 16 horsepower, was complemented by a steam engine in 1880 and later by electric power. The goods were bagged and taken away from the mill by cart or truck to the local railway station. Waste products from the process were bark, which was used in tanning, and 'wasters' which were sold as kindling wood.

Stott Mill survived making bobbins, reels, toggles and handles until the 1950s when the introduction of plastic brought about its demise. However, the site shows the variety of processes involved in making the product and the transportation and machinery needed to serve the industry.

Stott Park Bobbin Mill showing the raw material used.

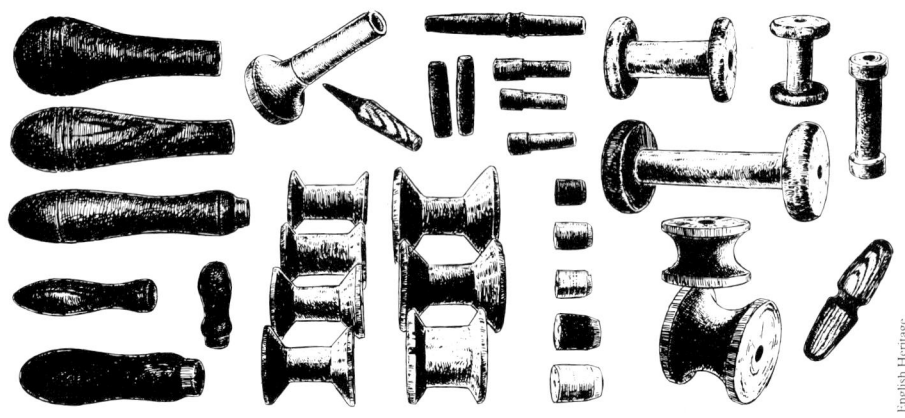

The wide range of products turned from coppice wood.

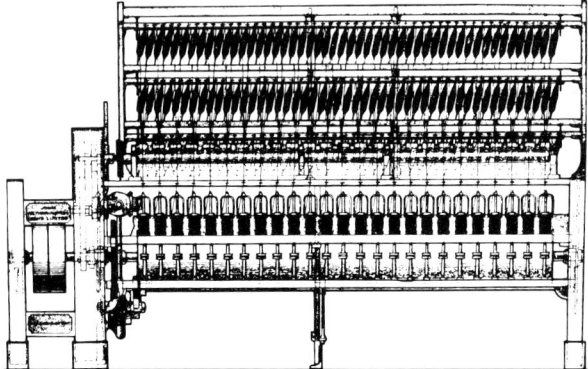

The growth of bobbin mills was initially to make bobbins for the new spinning and weaving machinery.

24

GEOGRAPHY AND THE HISTORIC ENVIRONMENT

SETTLEMENT SITES

This section contrasts two very different sites. Both show evidence of sequent occupation and the co-existence of different types of structure on the same site. The influence of early layout over the present shape of the settlement area can also be seen.

VILLAGE

Wharram Percy deserted village, North Yorkshire
(Map reference: SE 859645)

Wharram Percy lies near the north west scarp of the Yorkshire Wolds, about halfway between York and Scarborough. The main earthworks of the village are situated on the chalk plateau at about 150 metres above sea-level; in the valley is the church of St Martin and the site of the medieval fishpond. The village covers 13.4 hectares, and its associated field systems another 506 hectares. The village itself has undergone intensive archaeological excavation.

The area around Wharram has produced stone axes, some imported from the Lake District. On the plateau to the west of the village the hollows left by uprooted stumps indicate that the forest in the area was cleared about 3,500 BC by neolithic farmers. The earliest known houses were of an iron age date (c.100 BC), among them the home of a local chief. This was defended by a large ditch, and situated at the junction of three prehistoric earthworks. There was another settlement area by the stream. During the Roman period a series of farmsteads was built about 150 metres apart from the surrounding wolds. The wealthiest farm stood over the remains of the iron age defended homestead and may have been a villa, as its site has produced evidence of mosaic pavements and architectural stonework. Its timber outbuildings and corn drier have been excavated. The Roman land divisions may have influenced the siting of the later medieval properties, with the major medieval boundaries being based on Roman banks and ditches.

The Anglo-Saxon settlers of Wharram Percy may have continued to use parts of the existing farm systems, as Saxon finds have been located on the sites of three of the four Roman buildings. During late Saxon and early medieval times the settlement became nucleated, with the formation of a compact layout of houses around a clear street pattern. The new village at Wharram consisted of a regular street / green plan, with two parallel rows of tofts (houses and rear yards) and crofts (enclosed paddocks behind the houses) running north to south, a row to the north which runs east to west, and a triangular green enclosed by the rows of houses. The church lay in the southern part of the settlement near the mill and fishpond.

The layout of Wharram probably resulted from the unified scheme of one lord. By the time of the Domesday Survey in 1086, the village consisted of two manors; the original village plan may have been modified to include two manorial enclosures as important

(continued on page 28 ➤)

The late Saxon and medieval village of Wharram Percy (left).

A reconstruction drawing of Wharram Percy (below).

SETTLEMENT SITES

TOWN

York, North Yorkshire
(Centred on map reference: SE 605515)

The site of York is at the centre of a natural communications network with an easy east-west crossing of the low lying Vale of York, the tidal Ouse providing a link with the North Sea. It is also located where the river cuts through a glacial moraine that was used as an important routeway, and where the tributary River Foss joins the Ouse.

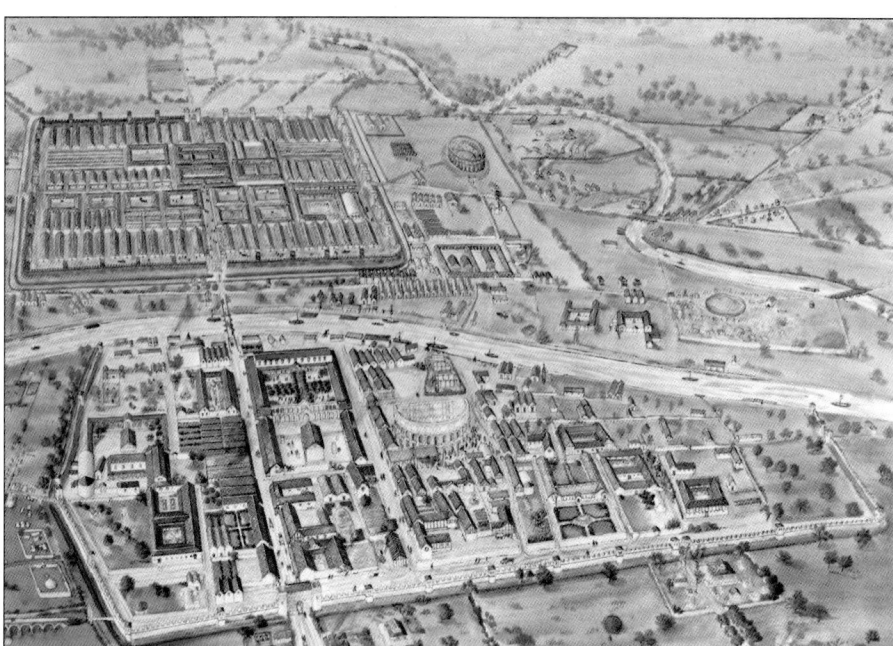

A reconstruction aerial drawing of York in 210 AD.

York city walls today.

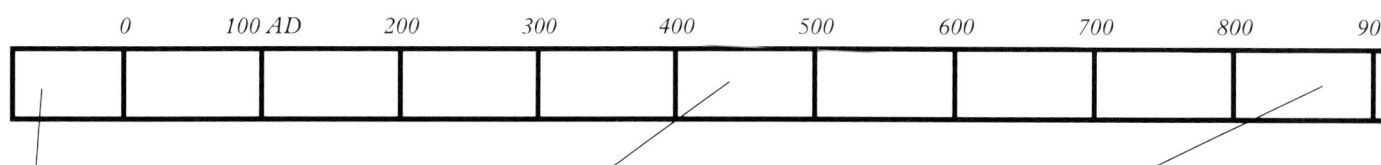

■ York began life as the legionary fortress of Eboracum, founded as the military capital of Britain, and headquarters of northern military command. The site was chosen for its river position; the river provided an alternative method of transport and a means of relieving the city if it was surrounded.

■ During the Anglian period some Roman buildings remained in good repair although the road network was not maintained. The city became the capital of King Edwin's kingdom of Northumbria, possibly because the surviving fortress walls were important for its defence - the walls were repaired twice in this period. The city was attracting trade, and several new churches were built to serve the growing population.

■ In AD 866 the Vikings seized York which they named Jorvik. The city prospered as trade grew, and it developed its own coin mint. The evidence of present street names with Norse elements such as 'gate' indicate that much of the modern city's layout was established in Viking Jorvik. Lines of property and of buildings set out in Jorvik did not change till modern times.

SETTLEMENT SITES

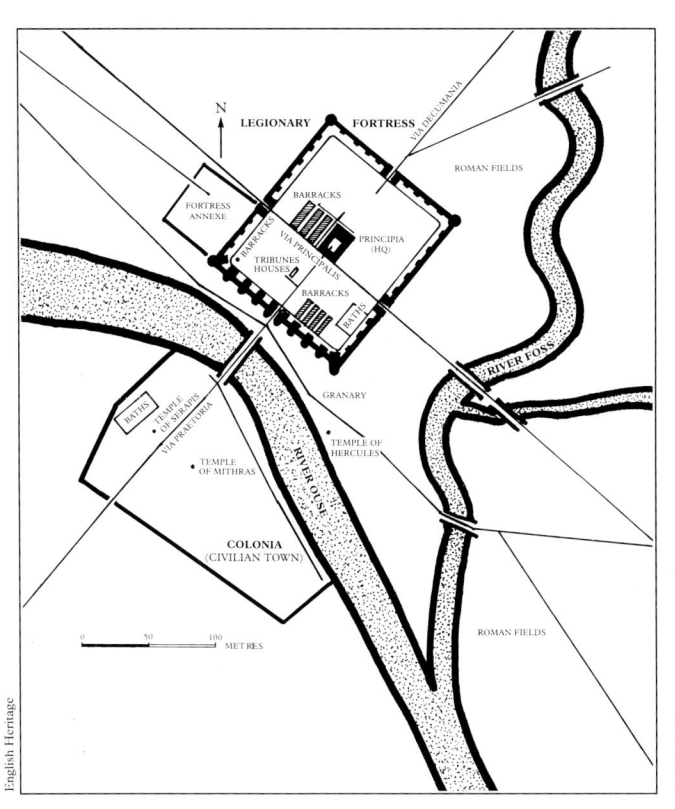

Roman York.

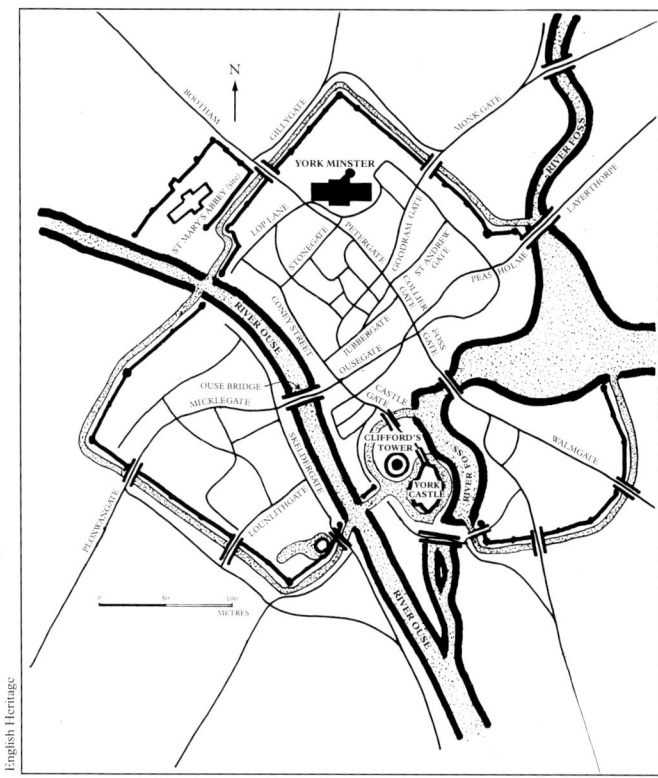

Medieval York.

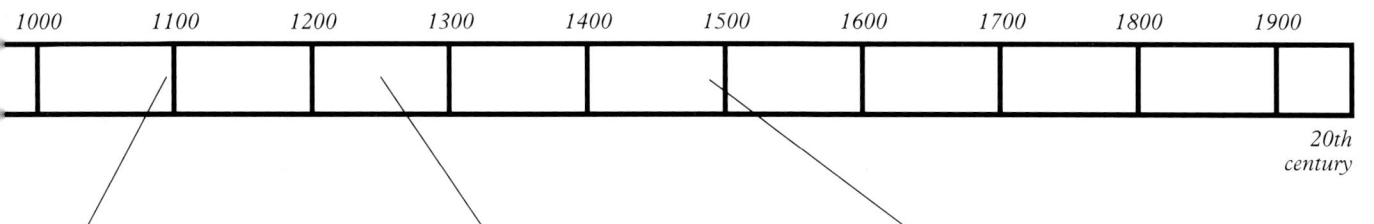

■ After the Norman Conquest half the city's dwellings were destroyed and two castles were built to control the inhabitants and help contain the region. These two castles were positioned either side of the River Ouse. The defences of the city were strengthened and heightened at this time and the principal gates to the city were refurbished or rebuilt. The abandonment of the Roman town plan can be seen in the placing of the Norman minster at an alignment of forty five degrees across the Roman fortress, although it was still on the site of the principia, or headquarters.

■ During the medieval period York ranked second only to London in terms of prosperity and political importance. By the mid thirteenth century the walls were being rebuilt in stone. The suburbs continued to develop as trading and manufacture grew along the roads entering the city. The wool trade was most important, but leather working, metal working, provision trades and the building industry were also prominent. The development of port facilities alongside the Ouse indicated the growth of external and foreign trade.

■ In the post medieval period York began to decline in importance. The collapse of the wool trade at the end of the fifteenth century and the eclipse of the city as a port by Hull both contributed to this decline. However by this time the layout of the city was established much as we see it today. The later growth of York as a railway centre did little to alter the townscape within the walls of the city. It is only recently that wholesale development has changed the medieval layout.

SETTLEMENT SITES

LINES OF ENQUIRY

What was this place like? Using a map or making fieldwork sketches:

■ Find the boundaries of the site; Does it have defences?

■ Where are the main routeways into the settlement? Are they protected by gates?

■ Find the main buildings and see how they relate to the street plan. Locate the centres of administration, such as castles, and areas associated with worship and ceremonial.

■ Research into the meaning of the street names to see if there is any connection with previous trades or physical features. Locate any areas associated with particular trades or industries.

■ Locate any central place that might have acted as a market place.

■ Which areas were used for houses?

Why was this place as it was? How and why did it differ from, or resemble other places?
Using the data gathered above try to answer a series of questions:

■ Why was the settlement sited here? How does it use the physical features of the site such as streams or rivers?

■ Are the streets laid out in a planned way or have they just developed? Are there any 'zones' for trades or commerce? Can you find any reason why a particular trade was started here?

■ Why did housing develop in a particular area?

■ How does the settlement compare to others in the locality or further afield? Was this settlement an important one on which others depended or did it depend on other settlements for instance, for trade or defence?

In what ways was this place connected to other places? Using fieldwork evidence and maps:

■ Where did the roads go to and what might have been transported on them? Was the river or stream used for transportation? Which routes were the main ones and went long distances, and which routes only served the locality?

■ Where is the nearest settlement of the same size and how is this settlement connected to it?

■ Are there any trade connections with other places?

How has this place changed and why?
Using fieldwork and guidebooks:

■ Is there any evidence that the settlement grew or shrank over time? What reasons were there for this?

■ Did the defences expand or did the settlement grow outside them? Did this happen in a certain direction?

■ How do earlier settlement patterns on the site influence later ones? When was the street plan formed and did it remain the same throughout time?

■ Did the purpose of the settlement change over time?

■ Did the types of trade change over time? Did areas for the administration of the settlement remain fixed or did they move to another part of the place? How did the area around the settlement change over time?

What would it have felt like to be in this place?

The information collected should allow the children to gain an impression of what it might have been like to live in the place when it was in use at a particular time.

■ Think about what you would have seen and felt at a particular part of the site.

■ Suggest what might have been happening at a particular location within the site at a particular time of the day or year.

Information gained from further work in the classroom will add to the children's impressions of the sites, particularly details of the attitudes, values and beliefs of its inhabitants.

(➤ *continued from page 25*)

central places. These changes of the tenth century also affected the surrounding countryside as it was divided in to a number of large fields and then subdivided into strips. Groups of these strips would have been farmed by different peasants. The result is usually seen in the landscape as ridge and furrow. The village was replanned when the two manors were combined in 1254.

The number of houses at Wharram Percy dropped from thirty in 1368 to only sixteen after 1435; the last was deserted about 1500. The reasons are complex. Land that had been intensively farmed for generations became exhausted and villages became uneconomic and were in decline even before the Black Death of the mid fourteenth century. In 1323 at Wharram two-thirds of the lord's lands were uncultivated, and his corn mills were derelict. A solution for the lord was to convert the fields to sheep pasture, as this required only a shepherd. This seems to have been what happened at Wharram with the unwanted labourers being evicted and the sites of the houses grassed over. The fields were let to a succession of sheep graziers.

The desertion of villages was not a rare occurrence; in the Midlands and Wolds areas up to one in six medieval villages is known to have been deserted for various reasons.

GEOGRAPHY AND THE HISTORIC ENVIRONMENT

CHANGE AND THE HISTORIC ENVIRONMENT

ROCHESTER UPON MEDWAY: A CASE STUDY

ELEMENTS OF THE PAST

Rochester upon Medway is renowned as an historic centre. It lies on the right bank of the river Medway at perhaps the lowest point that could have been used for a defensible crossing. Its sheltered anchorage so near the Thames has probably been the reason for its continued growth.

Visitors to the city today come to see the Norman cathedral, castle and town walls. There are buildings of historical and archaeological interest. These include Chertsey Gate, one of the old monastery's precinct gates; the Old Hall, a Tudor house with particularly fine wall-paintings, and Restoration House, an Elizabethan red-brick house where Charles II stayed in 1660 on his way to London to be crowned king.

The importance of the area in the defence of the River Thames and the south-east can be seen at Upnor Castle, a fortress built in the 1560s by Elizabeth I to protect the naval arsenal and dockyard at Chatham from attack by the sea; at Chatham Historic Dockyard, originating in the sixteenth century but described as the most complete eighteenth and early nineteenth century dockyard in the world, and Fort Amherst, the most complete eighteenth century fortress in Britain.

Visitors also come to Rochester to explore its connections with the Victorian novelist Charles Dickens, who lived there. Many of Dickens' novels use locations in the city.

However, these obvious signs of the activities of human beings in

Rochester Castle.

Rochester Cathedral.

the past are only part of the story. Much of the evidence of Rochester's past is hidden below the streets and surrounding countryside, for the area has a longer history than the earliest buildings that we can see. Within the town area, on gravels overlying the chalk, the earliest known permanent human occupation seems to have been just before the Roman invasion. Traces of a Belgic mint suggest that there was a settlement here of some importance possibly fortified by earthwork defences. Its Roman name, Durobrivae, meant 'the fort by the bridges'. The community developed along the road that we now call Watling Street. This was once the old trackway linking the Belgic sites of Canterbury and St. Albans, and forms the present High Street. The Roman town at Rochester, which may have been on the site of a Roman fort, grew with developing trade and towards the end of the second century AD it was fortified by an earth bank and ditch. Sometime in the next century a stone wall was built enclosing about ten hectares. This stone defence, and the pattern of streets inside it that have controlled the shape of the city through the Anglo-Saxon and Norman periods to the present day.

CHANGE AND THE HISTORIC ENVIRONMENT

THE INFLUENCE OF THE PAST

The 1:50 000 Ordnance Survey map of the Rochester area (The Thames Estuary, Sheet 178) contains many symbols for roads, motorways, quarries, bridges, and shows a large built up area that includes the castle, the cathedral, town walls and a considerable stretch of river side development of piers and docks. In the heart of the extensive stretches of woodland around Rochester there are archaeological sites showing that at one time those areas of land were open to some degree and that the present, often dense, covering of trees is no more than replantings in once open and inhabited sites.

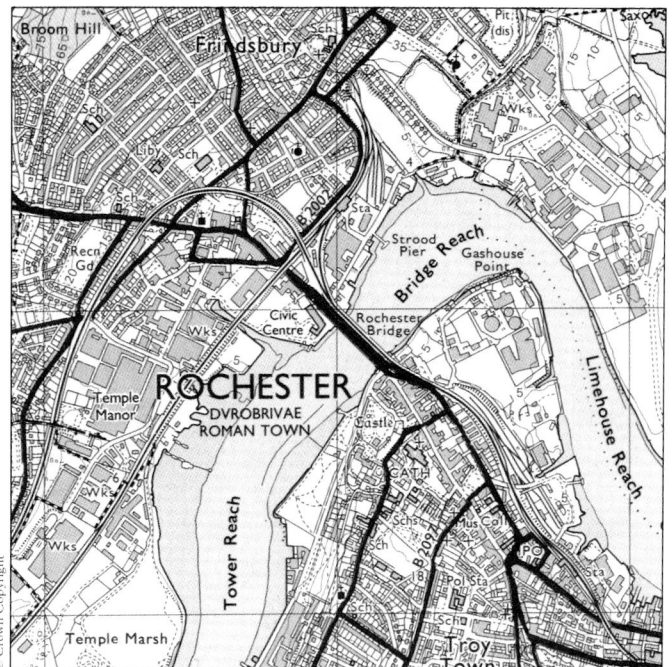

The Rochester area, shown on the 1:50 000 OS map.

The strategic position of Rochester Castle (below).

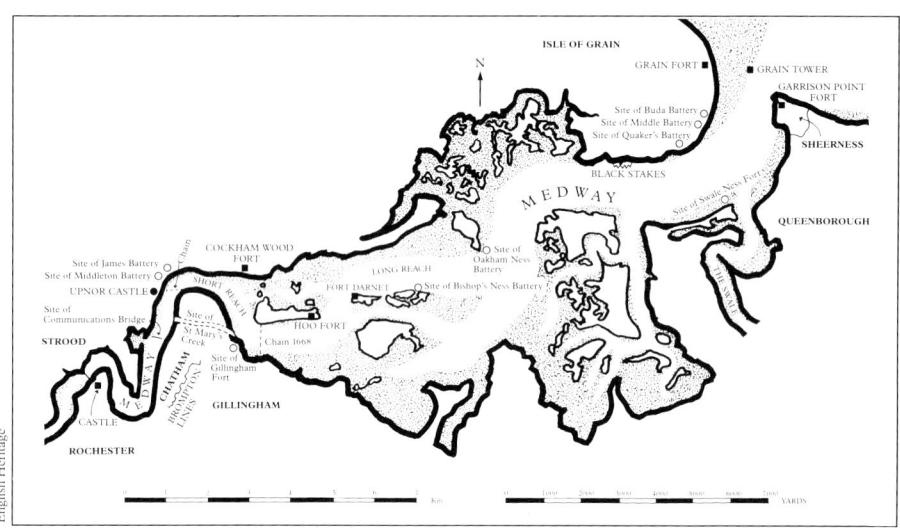

Fortifications on the River Medway. From the 16th century onwards fortifications were developed to protect the dockyard at Chatham.

Industry and its effect on the historic environment

Mining for flint may have occurred in the Rochester area in prehistoric times, for there are large areas of chalk around the town. With the discovery of the uses of metal for making more efficient tools and weapons came the exploration of ores and the further use of timber for fuel for smelting. The OS map indicates that there has been considerable mining around the Medway valley in the shape of quarries. With the growth of permanent settlement stone outcrops were used for building materials, and poorer quality rock and gravel has been quarried for use in roads and as foundations for buildings. The increased use of brick, particularly with the growth of the railways which made it easier to transport

ACTIVITY

■ Ask pupils to identify the most recent industrial or commercial development in the area of the school.

■ Using a variety of sources, including large-scale OS maps, Goad Street plans which show land use, and aerial photographs, ask pupils to find out what the new development replaced. This information may be plotted and overlaid on a current map of the area.

■ It should be possible to find out whether any historic features were destroyed to allow the new development to take place by reference to land use plans, old photographs and aerial views. Encourage pupils to compare road layouts as well as buildings.

■ Ask pupils to consider whether any historical features could have been incorporated into the development, perhaps with a different use.

■ If some buildings have been destroyed, was any record made of them before this happened?

CHANGE AND THE HISTORIC ENVIRONMENT

ACTIVITY

■ A questionnaire, devised to suit the particular site, will provide pupils with information about visitors and their impressions of the site.

■ Data collected in this way may be used to evaluate visitor facilities on offer, leading to pupils designing their own display panels, guidebook, refreshment area or visitor route for the site.

■ The data from the survey may also be used as a starting-point for an investigation into the site's impact on the local area. For example, if a large number of visitors arrive by car there may be parking and traffic flow problems. Pupils may be asked to consider where an additional car park could be located, bearing in mind constraints of access, landscaping and the conservation of any historic features.

■ Care should be taken when asking pupils to interview strangers. Pupils should work in groups of at least three and should avoid lonely places. They should be reminded about the need for courtesy when interviewing people. Role play exercises can be carried out in the classroom to prepare pupils for this activity.

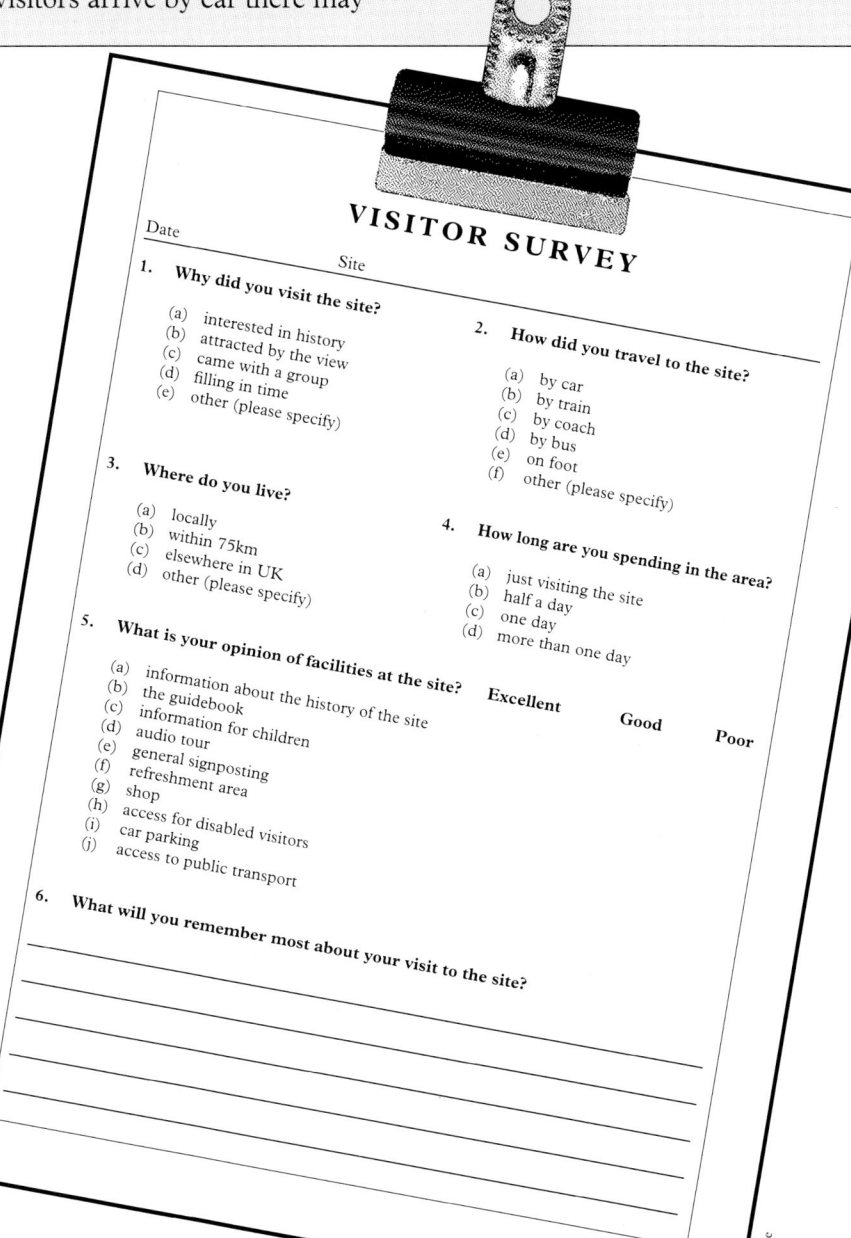

goods over long distances, has led to similar exploitation of the landscape. Industrial and agricultural activities which may damage or destroy archaeological sites include:

■ the development of deep ploughing techniques.

■ the removal of hedges which often marked ancient field boundaries.

■ open-cast mining and quarries for other minerals.

■ the routing of motorways and cross-country pipelines.

LINKS WITH OTHER PLACES

Tourism and the historic environment

Rochester upon Medway is easily accessible from London by rail or road and is a handy stopping-off point for visitors coming from the Channel ports.

Looking at the OS map it is clear that Rochester is no longer a pivotal point on the way to the Channel ports because the M2 motorway takes traffic around the city. With the closure of Chatham Naval Dockyard the Medway itself lost much of its role in Rochester's life. However, travellers still come to Rochester, but for different reasons. They

come to experience 'the heritage': the past of Rochester, the result of its past connections.

As we have seen Rochester has a high density of historic sites and museums. Many other historic areas throughout England share in this presentation of the past for the future. There is a new industry: the heritage industry and its new

CHANGE AND THE HISTORIC ENVIRONMENT

ACTIVITY

Ask pupils, working in pairs, to choose six buildings, structures or landscapes in the local area that they consider should be preserved for future generations. This may be done by visiting possible sites and drawing/photographing them, or it may be done by using visual and documentary sources in the classroom. Write the name of each building or structure on a separate postcard. (Each group will need six postcards).

For each building or site pupils should explain the reasons on which they based their decisions. They should then be asked to prioritise their choices one to six. For instance, pupils may consider

■ whether age in itself makes something worth preserving. If so, how old would the structure need to be?

■ should places be preserved because they look picturesque, or are industrial sites equally worth preserving?

■ whether the whole range of society and its activities is represented in the places chosen for preservation.

■ whether the needs of preservation should outweigh the needs of society for transport, industrial and leisure development for the future.

Each pair should then compare lists with another pair of pupils.

■ Were the same buildings chosen?.

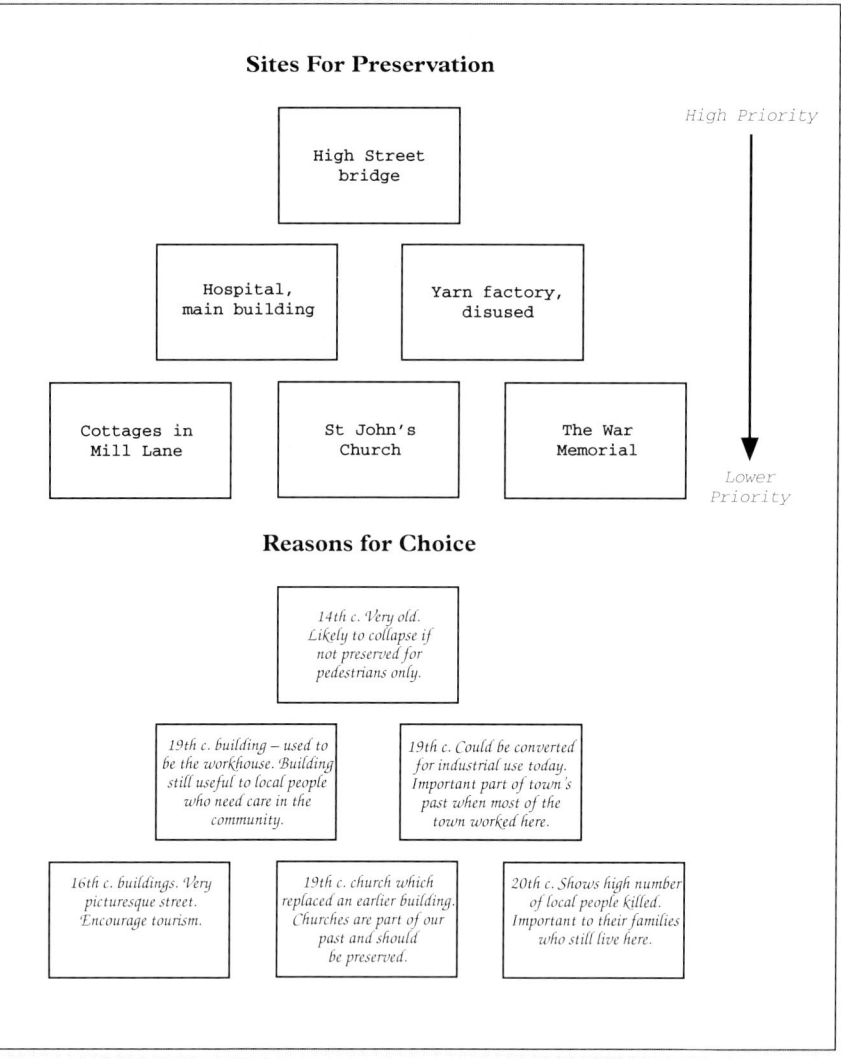

■ Were the reasons for choices similar?

■ Was the order of priority the same? If not, why did it differ? Were different reasons given more importance?

Ask each group of four to negotiate a list of only three buildings to be preserved with reasons. If this list is reported back to the whole class a picture should emerge of the similarities and differences of opinion over what is worth preserving and why. If only one of the buildings could be preserved, on what basis would the groups/class make this decision? At the end of this activity your pupils should be more aware of the different criteria for preservation of the historic environment, the differences in opinion that can affect decisions on preservation, and the possibilities of conflict between different criteria.

fields of study: Heritage Management, Cultural Resource Management and Heritage Education. The industry itself has given rise to other industries: there is a need for promotional literature, maps, postcards and souvenirs. A heritage site creates its own servicing needs.

The presence of a tourist attraction will have consequences for the local environment. The site itself is not only important for its past activity, it is important in the present geography of the landscape.

THE CHANGING ENVIRONMENT

We have seen how the city has changed through time to produce the urban landscape that we now experience as residents or visitors. Much of the evidence for change comes in the shape of historic documents, artefacts, pictures, or, for the more recent past, oral accounts. However, a major source of evidence is the structures themselves because they can give

CHANGE AND THE HISTORIC ENVIRONMENT

Chatham Dockyard.

us a real feeling for, as well as information on, how people in the past spent their lives.

Children are very aware of environmental and conservation issues which are often concerned with the wise use of finite resources and the protection of natural habitats. However we have come to realise that historic sites are also a non-renewable resource.

Conservation of the past

The historic environment is as worthy of protection as the natural environment. Sometimes priorities that are concerned with our present communications network or industrial needs take precedence over the protection of the historic environment, but often it is possible to save a site for the present and succeeding generations of people.

The two main methods of protection are the scheduling of sites, and the listing of buildings. A site or building may be of national importance because it is the only example of a type of site or an architect's work. It may be an important element in a landscape or townscape that is worth preserving. Not all sites are ancient, some sites and buildings from the recent past are also being preserved as they are seen as not only important now but as being increasingly important in the future. Not all preserved sites are scenic; some are industrial. Whole areas of archaeological importance are also protected as well as the remains of individual structures.

ACTIVITY

Pupils could be asked to survey a small section of one of the streets of Rochester, or any other historic town, to identify evidence of the past that remains today.

■ Ask pupils to look for changes in the use of buildings: old shopsigns painted high on walls often give a clue here. Additions and alterations to buildings resulting from change of use can be noted.

■ Open spaces in a built up area may reflect a past event or past use; for example an old market area no longer used and turned into a car park, or a small garden on the site of a building destroyed during the Second World War.

■ Street names are also a fertile source of information. These details may be recorded in a set of annotated photographs or a slide sequence with accompanying commentary.

■ The position of the noted buildings or areas may be marked on a street plan of the area, in varying degrees of detail. For instance buildings or remains from different periods or buildings of differing use - domestic, industrial, commercial - may be noted in different colours.

33

CHANGE AND THE HISTORIC ENVIRONMENT

There are approximately 13,000 scheduled ancient monuments, and 440,000 listed buildings in England.

Since 1967 local authorities have had powers to designate conservation areas. Specific consent is required to demolish buildings, fell trees, or make alterations that would change the character of these areas. Some historic places have been designated World Heritage Sites; Stonehenge in its landscape is one of these. National Parks and Areas of Outstanding Natural Beauty are two further categories aimed at protecting the natural landscape from further development.

There are also many organisations who are concerned with promoting protection of sites and buildings including English Heritage; the Council for British Archaeology; the Council for the Preservation of Rural England; the National Trust; and the Society for the Protection of Ancient Buildings.

At Rochester the castle is preserved by English Heritage as a scheduled ancient monument, as are the surrounding historic sites of Upnor Castle, Milton Chantry and Temple Manor. The Chatham Historic Dockyard Trust, formed in 1984, has 47 scheduled ancient monuments on its 80 acre site. Many of the buildings in Rochester are listed but are looked after by the city itself or by private trusts and charities.

Whole areas of landscape which have visible evidence of human activity are also considered to have an environmental quality that is worth preserving. The layouts of our medieval towns, where they survive as in Rochester, York or Hereford, also enhance an area of land. Where they have been largely destroyed to cope with motor traffic this is usually regretted. At Rochester the main traffic bypasses the historic core of the city and the old High Street, which follows the line of the ancient Watling Street, is now a pedestrian shopping area.

Change of use

In Rochester there are many places that are a product of the past and are still used for the same purposes in the present. The cathedral is a good example of this. It has been used for worship since the Norman conquest and whilst it does attract tourists, it remains primarily a place of sanctity and prayer. However, in our fast-moving society it is unusual to find historic structures beyond those used for religious purposes that retain their original function.

This chapel was built in 1863. This photograph was taken in 1973.

The chapel was then converted into a house, changing the building dramatically. This photograph was taken in 1991.

This supermarket in Carnforth, Lancashire was originally the local cinema.

ACTIVITY

Locate and map historic buildings in your locality that are used for purposes different from their original functions. Identify the characteristics of the individual building that make it especially appropriate for its new use. Consider for instance, window size, height of internal ceilings, proximity to main roads, number of entrances to the building, and aesthetic features.

Religious buildings, because of their solidity and historic qualities are often also used in other ways. Chapels as warehouses, churches as offices, private homes, art galleries or shops are examples frequently seen. Redundant school buildings are often used as offices or industrial units.

GEOGRAPHY AND THE HISTORIC ENVIRONMENT

BIBLIOGRAPHY AND RESOURCES

BIBLIOGRAPHY

Books for Teachers

General Reference
M. Aston, **Interpreting the Landscape,** Batsford, 1985, ISBN 0-7134-3650-6

T. Darvill, **Ancient Monuments in the Countryside,** English Heritage, 1987, ISBN 1-85074-167-0

T. Darvill, **Prehistoric Britain,** Batsford, 1992, ISBN 0-7134-5180-7

R.A. Dodgshon and R.A. Butlin, **An Historical Geography of England and Wales,** Academic Press, 1990, ISBN 0-12-219254-0

W.G. Hoskins, **Fieldwork in Local History,** Faber and Faber, 1982, ISBN 0-571-18051-5

W.G. Hoskins, **The Making of the English Landscape,** Hodder & Stoughton, 1992, ISBN 0-340-56648-5

R. Muir, **Reading the Landscape,** Michael Joseph, 1981, ISBN 0-7181-1971-1

O. Rackham, **The History of the Countryside,** Dent, 1989, ISBN 0-460-12552-4

D. Smith, **Maps and Plans for the Local Historian and Collector,** Batsford, 1988, ISBN 0-7134-5191-2

J.M. Wagstaff(Ed), **Landscape and Culture: Geographical and Archaeological Perspectives,** Basil Blackwell, 1987, ISBN 0-631-15288-1

D.R. Wilson, **Air Photo Interpretation for Archaeologists,** Batsford, 1982, ISBN 0-7134-1086-8

J.B. Whittow, **Landscape of Stone,** Whittet Books, 1986, ISBN 0-905483-50-2

R.J. Woodell, **The English Landscape, Past, Present, and Future,** Oxford University Press, 1985, ISBN 0-19-21-1621-5

Ed Halkon, Corbishley and Binns, **The Archaeology Resource Book,** English Heritage / Council for British Archaeology, 1992, ISBN 1-872414-18-4

Defensive sites
R. Allen Brown, **Castles,** Shire Archaeology, 1985, ISBN 0-85263-653-9

T. Copeland, **A Teachers' Guide to Using Castles,** English Heritage (to be published 1993)

B. Cunliffe, **Danebury, The Anatomy of an Iron Age Hillfort,** Batsford, 1983, ISBN 0-7134-0998-3

S. Johnson, **Hadrian's Wall,** English Heritage/Batsford, 1989 ISBN 0-7134-5958-1

T. McNeill, **Castles,** English Heritage/Batsford, 1992, ISBN 0-7134-7025-9

N. Sharples, **Maiden Castle,** English Heritage/Batsford, 1991, ISBN 0-7134-6083-0

A. Saunders, **Fortress Britain: Artillery Fortification in the British Isles and Ireland,** Beaufort Publishing, 1989, ISBN 1-85512-000-3

H. Wills, **Pillboxes: A study of UK Defences 1940,** Leo Cooper, 1985, ISBN 0-436-57360-1

Rural sites
M. Girouard, **Life in the English Country House,** Penguin Books, 1980, ISBN 0-14-005406-5

R. Muir, **The Lost Villages of Britain,** Michael Joseph, 1986, ISBN 0-7181-2784-6

B.K. Roberts, **Village Plans,** Shire Books, 1982, ISBN 0-85263-601-6

T. Rowley, **Villages in the Landscape,** Alan Sutton, 1987, ISBN 0-86299-448-9

T. Rowley and J. Wood, **Deserted Villages,** Shire Books, ISBN 0-85263-5931

C. Taylor, **Fields in the English Landscape,** Alan Sutton, 1987, ISBN 0-86299-44-9

M. Wood, **The English Medieval House,** Dent, 1965, ISBN 0-46007-813-5

Religious sites
C. Cooksey, **A Teachers' Guide to Using Abbeys,** English Heritage, 1992, ISBN 1-85074-297-9

G. Coppack, **Abbeys and Priories,** English Heritage/Batsford, 1990, ISBN 0-7134-6308-2

R. Morris, **Churches in the Landscape,** Dent, 1989, ISBN 0-460-04509-1

W. Rodwell, **Church Archaeology,** English Heritage/Batsford, 1989, ISBN 0-7134-6293-0

Industry
K. Hudson, **The Archaeology of Industry,** The Bodley Head, 1976, ISBN 0-370-01591-6

B. Trinder, **The Making of the Industrial Landscape,** Alan Sutton, 1987, ISBN 0-86299-445-4

Settlement sites
M. Atkin and K. Thompson, **Revealing Lost Villages, Wharram Percy,** English Heritage, 1986, ISBN 1-85074-121-2

M. Aston and J. Bond, **The Landscape of Towns,** Alan Sutton, 1987, ISBN 0-86299-450-0

M. Beresford and J. Hurst, **Wharram Percy: Deserted Medieval Village,** English Heritage/Batsford, 1990, ISBN 0-7134-6114-4

M. Carver, **Underneath English Towns,** Batsford, 1987, ISBN 0-7134-3638-7

C. Keith, **A Teachers' Guide to Using Listed Buildings,** English Heritage, 1991, ISBN 1-85074-297-9

English Heritage Handbooks for Teachers: These handbooks for specific sites help teachers to plan a visit. They give the historical background and a variety of study approaches which include documentary sources and activity sheets for classroom and on-site work together with practical information about the site.

For a full list of Teachers' Handbooks, see our 'Resources' catalogue.

BIBLIOGRAPHY AND RESOURCES

Children's Books
Among the large number of children's books on the historic environment the following are particularly useful.

E. Allen, **Building and History: Industry,** Black, 1977, ISBN 0-7136-1758-6

L. Bolwell and C. Lines, **The Countryside in the Past,** Wayland, 1987, ISBN 0-85078-933-8

S. Buxton, T. Copeland and C. Shephard, **Castles and Cathedrals,** John Murray, 1992, ISBN 0-7195-4952-3

R. Christian, **Factories, Forges and Foundries,** Routledge and Kegan Paul, 1974, ISBN 0-7100-7901

P. Connolly, **The Roman Fort,** Oxford University Press, 1991, ISBN 0-19-917108-4

M. Corbishley, **The Middle Ages: Cultural Atlas for Young People,** Facts on File, 1990, ISBN 0-8160-1973-8

B. Davison, **A Place in the Country: Roman Villa,** Hamish Hamilton, 1984, ISBN 0-241-11241-9

B. Davison, **Looking at a Castle,** Kingfisher, 1987, ISBN 0-86272-251-9

B. Davison, **The New Observers Book of Castles,** Fredrick Warne, 1988, ISBN 0-7232-3339-X

W. Farnworth, **Industry,** Mills and Boon, 1977, ISBN 0-263-05585-0

P and H. Speed, **The Industrial Revolution,** Oxford, 1985, ISBN 0-19-917061-3

G. Thie, **Living in the Past - The Middle Ages,** Blackwell, ISBN 0-631-91140-5

R. Whitlock, **Exploring Buildings,** Wayland, 1987, ISBN 1-85210-002-8

R. Whitlock, **Landscape in History,** Wayland, 1984, ISBN 0-85078-452-2

AUDIO-VISUAL RESOURCES

Castles and Later Fortifications, English Heritage Nine full colour aerial photographs posters with notes for teachers and suggested book lists.
Medieval Castles of Britain, 100 colour slides available from Focal Point Audio-Visual Ltd, 251, Copnor Rd, Portsmouth, PO3 5EE.

Videos
Your Church: a threshold to history, English Heritage, 1987, 23 minutes. a guide to what you can observe and interpret from an ordinary parish church. Available from English Heritage Postal Sales.
Evidence of our lives, English Heritage, 1991, 27 minutes. This video shows how children can develop skills by recording, researching and interpreting their local environment. Available from English Heritage Postal Sales.
Looking at a Castle, English Heritage, 1980 Uses the remains at Goodrich Castle to explain the complex arrangements of life in a medieval castle through investigations of clues left behind in the building. Available from English Heritage Postal Sales.
The Norman Conquest of England, English Heritage 1982 This video shows how the Norman Conquest of England altered not only building styles, but our landscape and language as well. Available from English Heritage Postal Sales: English Heritage, PO Box 229, Northampton NN6 9RY.

Maps
The Ordnance Survey publishes several useful historic maps including
Roman and Anglian York, Ordnance Survey, ISBN 0-31929-0174, 1:2500 scale
Viking and Medieval York, Ordnance Survey, ISBN 0-31929-0166, 1:2500 scale
Roman and Medieval Bath, Ordnance Survey, ISBN 0-31929-0220, 1:2500 scale
Georgian Bath, Ordnance Survey, ISBN 0-31929-0239, 1:2500 scale
Roman and Medieval Canterbury, Ordnance Survey, ISBN 0-31929-0263, 1:2500 scale
Roman London (Londinuim), Ordnance Survey, ISBN 0-31929-0158, 1:2500 scale
Ancient Britain, Ordnance Survey, ISBN 0-31929-0018, 1:625000 scale
Roman Britain, Ordnance Survey, ISBN 0-31929-0255, 1:625000 scale
Hadrian's Wall, Ordnance Survey, ISBN 0-31929-0182, 1:50000 or 1:12500 scale
Bodleian Map of Great Britain (The Gough Map), Ordnance Survey, ISBN 0-31900-9033

A reproduction of the Bodleian Library's medieval map of Great Britain, circa A.D 1360.

Copies of old maps
Although Ordnance Survey does not hold a complete set, the majority of its old maps are still available, from which black and white copies can be supplied. Contact Ordnance Survey Special Products Department. Tel: 0703-792338.
David and Charles (Brunel House, Newton Abbott, Devon) publishes a complete reprint of Victorian Ordnance Survey maps from 1805 to 1873, covering England and Wales in 97 sheets.

ACKNOWLEDGEMENTS
Thanks to pupils of St Peter's Methodist Primary School, Canterbury and to Bryony Stephen, for their maps and cross sections.

English # Heritage

Schools can make a free educational visit to any English Heritage Historic Property provided this is pre-booked through the relevant regional office at least two weeks in advance. Teachers can also arrange a free exploratory visit beforehand to prepare ideas for the main visit later. The Education Service aims to provide teachers with as much help as possible to use the resource of the historic environment. If you have any requests for further information please contact us at:
**English Heritage
Education Service
Keysign House
429 Oxford Street
London W1R 2HD
Tel: 071-973 3442/3
Fax: 071-973 3430**